AF392727

Towards the Sun
The Mother on Egypt

✴

Queen Hatshepsut, Queen Tiye & Queen Cleopatra
from
Akhet-Aten (Tell el-Amarna), Egypt
to Auroville, India

Franz Fassbender

Acknowledgement

All texts of Sri Aurobindo and The Mother are the copyright of the Sri Aurobindo Ashram Trust, Pondicherry, India with the exception of the texts from Mother's Agenda, © The copyright holder for Mother's Agenda is "Institut de Recherches Evolutives".

Towards the Sun
The Mother on Egypt
Copyright : Prisma, Auroville
Author : Franz Fassbender

Second revised edition 2023

ISBN 978-93-95460-65-1 (Paperpack)
ISBN 978-93-95460-99-6 (ebook)

BISAC Code:
TRV015010, TRAVEL / Middle East / Egypt
LCO000000, LITERARY COLLECTIONS / General
LCO022030, LITERARY COLLECTIONS / Subjects & Themes / Places *
REL033000, RELIGION / History
EDU000000, EDUCATION / General
EDU043000, EDUCATION / Comparative
EDU016000, EDUCATION / History
HIS062000, HISTORY / Asia / South / India
HIS037070, HISTORY / Modern / 20th Century / General
HIS003000, History / Asia / General
HIS030000, HISTORY / Reference

Thema Subject Category:
NKD, Archaeology by period / region
1QBAE, Ancient Egypt
BS, Social groups, communities and identities
NH, History
NHF, Asian history
NHT, History: specific events and topics
NHTB, Social and cultural history
NK , Archaeology

Cataloging-in-Publication Data for this title is available from the Library of Congress.

Published by:
PRISMA, an imprint of Digital Media Initiatives
PRISMA, Aurelec / Prayogshala, Auroville 605101, Tamil Nadu, India
www.prisma.haus

A note on The Mother

The Mother was born Mirra Alfassa on February 21st, 1878, in Paris. A student at the Academie Julian, she became an accomplished artist. Gifted from an early age with a capacity for spiritual and occult experiences, she went to Tlemcen, Algeria, in 1906 and 1907 to study occultism with the adept Max Théon and his wife.

Between 1911 and 1913 she gave a number of talks to various groups of seekers in Paris, and began to record her deepening communion with the Divine in the diary later published as *Prayers and Meditations.*

In 1914 the Mother voyaged to Pondicherry, South India, to meet the Indian mystic Sri Aurobindo. After a stay of eleven months, she was obliged by the outbreak of the First World War to return to France. A year later she went to Japan, where she remained for four years.

In 1920 the Mother rejoined Sri Aurobindo in Pondicherry. Six years later, when the Sri Aurobindo Ashram was founded, Sri Aurobindo entrusted its material and spiritual charge to her, for he considered her not a disciple but his spiritual equal and collaborator. Under her guidance the Ashram grew into a large, many-faceted spiritual community.

She also established a school, the Sri Aurobindo International Centre of Education, in 1952, and the international township of Auroville in 1968.

Auroville celebrated in 2018 its 50th Anniversary.

The Mother's teachings have been published in the *Collected Works of the Mother,* which to date comprise 17 volumes. Additionally, in *Mother's Agenda,* a 13-volume record of her conversations with her disciple Satprem, the Mother also gave a detailed account of her exploration into the body-consciousness, and her discovery of a "cellular mind" capable of restructuring the nature of the body and the laws of the species.

The Mother passed away on November 17th, 1973.

Introduction

The earliestrecord we have of Mother speaking of Queen Tiye is her conversation with Satprem on 5th June 1965, published in *Mother's Agenda* Vol. 6.

In April 1989 the monthly Auroville magazine *Auroville Today* published an article by Gilbert Lachaux titled "Auroville Yesterday". This was the first time somebody made the connection of the two cities Akhet-Aten (Tell el-Amarna) and Auroville. The article was based on the book *Nefertiti et le rêve d'Akhenaton* by Andrée Chedid.

In the year 2000 Aurovilian writer Georges Van Vrekhem published his book *The Mother: The Story of Her Life.* In this book the author writes extensively on Mother's reincarnations as Queen Hatshepsut and Queen Tiye.

In the same year 2000, the Laboratory of Evolution (LOE) in Auroville published a booklet called "AKHETATON & AUROVILLE: Towards the Sun (Vers Le Soleil)", a research document by Claire Le Touzé. This publication made available for the first time all the material on the connection between Akhet-Aten and Auroville.

2008, Paul Vincent Baptiste published the book: "Sur les Sentiers Solaires (On the Solar Path), Ou l'Histoire pas comme les autres".

Now, after 23 years, much more documentation is available, bringing back from history "Egypt's Golden Couple", when Akhenaten and Nefertiti were Gods on Earth.

Akhet-Aten (Tell el-Amarna) has become a well researched place in Egypt, but the connection to Auroville, India and The Mother, Mirra Alfassa, is still a story not many know about.

This compilation now tries to collect all the material available, and make known what connects the abandoned, destroyed and buried city of Akhet-Aten ("Horizon of the Aten"), at the site called Tell el-Amarna on the Nile River, with the growing new city of Auroville, dedicated to Human Unity, founded in 1968 near Pondicherry, South India.

The first chapters of this bring some light from Sri Aurobindo on how the Universe was created and on the cyclical nature of evolution. These views were expressed by the ancient Indian Rishis in the Vedas and Upanishads, using a similar symbolism as was used in Egypt, as we will see.

The time of Queen Hatshepsut (1473 – 1458 BCE), Queen Tiye and Akhenaten (1352 – 1336 BCE.) was indeed a pivotal point in history and evolution on this planet. In the Mother's most recent incarnation (1878 – 1973 C.E.), she again accelerated the evolution of humanity and the growth of consciousness upon earth. Mother and Sri Aurobindo through the whole of their lives, actions and achievements formed and lived the perfect symbiosis of Male and Female divine consciousness. The connection to ancient Egypt will help us to understand Mother's vast role as a creator in a much greater picture.

Satprem asks "Who was the Mother?" And he answers:

"She was the Ancient One of evolution who had come to make a new cleft in the old, tedious habit of being a man... She was the adventuress par excellence – the adventuress of the earth… She was there to discover ... the new species ... a new Matter ... a new Spirit."

The Mother herself describes her role: "Since the beginning of the earth, wherever and whenever there was the possibility of manifesting a ray of the Consciousness, I was there."

Contents

Remembering Queen Hatshepsut

Akhet-Aten

The Mother remembers

Auroville

Hymn to Surya

GLOWING like the red passion-flower,

born of the Supreme Light,

lo, the Mighty Splendour!

He dispels darkness, he slays

all ills, I bow to the

creator of the Day.

Nolini Kanta Gupta

Lift your eyes towards the Sun

Sri Aurobindo, Isha Upanishad

THE GURU

... Lift your eyes towards the Sun; He is there in that wonderful heart of life & light and splendour. Watch at night the innumerable constellations glittering like so many solemn watchfires of the Eternal in the limitless silence which is no void but throbs with the presence of a single calm and tremendous existence; see there Orion with his sword and belt shining as he shone to the Aryan fathers ten thousand years ago at the beginning of the Aryan era, Sirius in his splendour, Lyra sailing billions of miles away in the ocean of space.

Remember that these innumerable worlds, most of them mightier than our own, are whirling with indescribable speed at the beck of that Ancient of Days whither none but He knoweth, and yet that they are a million times more ancient than your Himalaya, more steady than the roots of your hills, and shall so remain until He at his will shakes them off like withered leaves from the eternal tree of the Universe.

Imagine the endlessness of Time, realise the boundlessness of Space, and then remember that when these worlds were not, He was, the Same as now, and when these are not, He shall be, still the Same; perceive that beyond Lyra He is and far away in Space where the stars of the Southern Cross cannot be seen, still He is there.

And then come back to the Earth & realise who this He is. He is quite near to you. See yonder old man who passes near you crouching & bent, with his stick.

Do you realise that it is God who is passing? There a child runs laughing in the sunlight. Can you hear Him in that laughter? Nay, He is nearer still to you. He is in you, He is you. It is yourself that burns yonder millions of miles away in the infinite reaches of Space, that walks with confident steps on the tumbling billows of the ethereal sea; it is you who have set the stars in their places and woven the necklace of the suns not with hands but by that Yoga, that silent actionless impersonal Will which has set you here today listening to yourself in me.

Look up, O child of the ancient Yoga, and be no longer a trembler and a doubter; fear not, doubt not, grieve not; for in your apparent body is One who can create & destroy worlds with a breath.

Sri Aurobindo, Isha Upanishad, CWSA 17, pp 130-132

Hymn to Dawn

Translation by Nolini Kanta Gupta

RIGVEDA
Mandala I: Sukta 92

Easily they rise up, the glowing rays; they yoke the luminous herds and yoke them perfectly. As of yore the Dawns give forms to the perception, the bright rays merge in the blazing Sun.

✷

Lo, her shining flame is before us: it is there spreading wide, holding back the mass of darkness. The Daughter of Heaven displays in our knowings the solar rays as though her own limbs and then merges in the glory of the Sun.

✷

We have crossed over to the other shore of this Darkness. Dawn breaks out and creates all manifested form. She smiles as with the beauty of poetic rhythm. She shines out with her perfect face. She unveils herself and brings to us a happy mind.

✷

Luminous she leads forth the blissful truths. Daughter of Heaven she is hymned by the most enlightened: O Dawn, bestow upon us all the plenitudes of progeny and the hero-power and the lifeforce-consciousness and the herd with the front of light.

O Dawn, may I enjoy that wealth full of glory and perfect hero-strength and the great host of servitors and the wakeful vital force. Thou bringest forth the plenitude, O Goddess of perfect enjoyment; thou shinest with the hearing perfect in action. Vast is that wealth of thine.

*

She takes birth again and again and shines with the same beauty of hue as of old. She, the Goddess, like a cutter slays the morrow of creatures and diminishes the life-span of aging mortals.

*

Lo! The luminous Goddess of Delight spreading out like a herd of kine! Like a river She extends herself wide over low lands. She never impairs the Divine Works, she awakes and becomes visible with the rays of the Sun.

*

O Dawn, break forth for us here today with thy light and energy and lustre and joy and the blissful Truth.

*

O Dawn, Goddess of Plenitude, yoke the luminous life-forces and bring to us all the felicities (perfect enjoyings).

*

May the wakers in the Dawn bring here for drinking the soma-wine the twin-gods who create delight, who do the work and follow the golden path.

Nolini Kanta Gupta, Collected Works, Book 8, p.10

The Beginning and the End

Sri Aurobindo, Essays Divine and Human

Who knows the beginning of things or what mind has ever embraced their end? When we have said a beginning, do we not behold spreading out beyond it all the eternity of Time when that which has begun was not?

So also when we imagine an end our vision becomes wise of endless Space stretching out beyond the terminus we have fixed. Do even forms begin and end? Or does eternal Form only disappear from one of its canvases?

The experiment of human life on an earth is not now for the first time enacted. It has been conducted a million times before and the long drama will again a million times be repeated. In all that we do now, our dreams, our discoveries, our swift or difficult attainments we profit subconsciously by the experience of innumerable precursors and our labour will be fecund in planets unknown to us and in worlds yet uncreated.

The plan, the peripeties, the denouement differ continually, yet are always governed by the conventions of an eternal Art. God, Man, Nature are the three perpetual symbols.

The idea of eternal recurrence affects with a shudder of alarm the mind entrenched in the minute, the hour, the years, the centuries, all the finite's unreal defences. But the strong soul conscious of its own immortal stuff and the inexhaustible ocean of its ever-flowing energies is seized by it with the thrill of an inconceivable rapture.

It hears behind the thought the childlike laughter and ecstasy of the Infinite.

God, Man, Nature, what are these three? Whence flow their divergences? To what ineffable union advances the ever-increasing sum of their contacts?

Let us look beyond the hours and moments; let us tear down the hedge of the years and the concept-wall of centuries and millenniums and break out beyond the limits of our prison-house. For all things seek to concentrate our view on the temporal interests, conceptions and realisations of our humanity.

We have to look beyond them to know that which they serve and represent. Nothing in the world can be understood by itself, but only by that which is beyond it. If we would know all, we must turn our gaze to that which is beyond all. That being known all else is comprehended.

✳

A beginningless and endless eternity and infinity in which divisible Time and Space manage to subsist is the mould of existence.

They succeed in subsisting because they are upheld by God's view of Himself in things.

God is all existence. Existence is a representation of ineffable Being. Being is neither eternal nor temporary, neither infinite nor limited, neither one nor many; it is nothing that any word of our speech can describe nor any thought of our mentality can conceive. The word existence unduly limits it; eternity & infinity are too petty conceptions; the term Being is an x representing not an unknown but an unknowable value. All values proceed from the Brahman, but it is itself beyond all values.

This existence is an incalculable Fact in which all possible opposites meet; its opposites are in truth identities.

It is neither one nor many and yet both one and many.

Numberlessness increases in it and extends till it reaches unity; unity broken cannot stop short of numberlessness.

It is neither personal nor impersonal and yet at once personal and impersonal. Personality is a fiction of the impersonal; impersonality the mask of a Person. That impersonal Brahman was all the time a world-transcendent Personality and universal Person, is the truth of things as it is represented by life and consciousness.

"I am" is the eternal assertion. Analytic thought gets rid of the I, but the Am remains and brings it back.

Materialism changes "I am" into "It is", and when it has done so, has changed nothing. The Nihilist gets rid of both Am and Is only to find them waiting for him beyond on either side of his negation.

When we examine the Infinite and the Finite, Form and the Formless, the Silence and the Activity, our oppositions are equally baffled. Try however hard we will, God will not allow us to exclude any of them from His fathomless universality. He carries all Himself with Him into every transcendence.

✸

As all words come out of the Silence, so all forms come out of the Infinite.

When the word goes back into the silence is it extinct for ever or does it dwell in the eternal harmony? When a soul goes back to God is it blotted out from existence or does it know and enjoy that into which it enters?

Does universe ever end? Does it not exist eternally in God's total idea of His own being?

Unless the Eternal is tired out by Time as by a load, unless God suffers loss of memory, how can universe cease from being?

Neither for soul nor universe is extinction the goal, but for one it is infinite self-possessing and for the other the endless pursuit of its own immutably mutable rhythms.

*

Existence, not annihilation is the whole aim and pursuit of existence.

If Nothing were the beginning Nothing also would be the end; but in that case Nothing also would be the middle.

If indiscriminable unity were the beginning it would also be the end. But then what middle term could there be except indiscriminable unity?

There is a logic in existence from which our Thought tries to escape by twisting and turning against its own ultimate necessity, as if a snake were to try to get away from itself by coiling round its own body. Let it cease coiling and go straight to the root of the whole matter, that there is no first nor last, no beginning nor ending, but only a representation of successions and dependences.

Succession and dependence are laws of perspective; they cannot be made a true measure of that which they represent.

Precisely because God is one, indefinable and beyond form, therefore He is capable of infinite definition and quality, realisation in numberless forms and the joy of endless self-multiplication. These two things go together and they cannot really be divided.

Sri Aurobindo, Essays Divine and Human with Thoughts and Aphorisms

Human History and Spiritual Evolution

There have been times when the seeking for spiritual attainment was, at least in certain civilisations, more intense and widespread than now or rather than it has been in the world in general during the past few centuries.

For now the curve seems to be the beginning of a new turn of seeking which takes its start from what was achieved in the past and projects itself towards a greater future.

But always, even in the age of the Vedas or in Egypt, the spiritual achievement or the occult knowledge was confined to a few; it was not spread in the whole mass of humanity. The mass of humanity evolves slowly, containing in itself all stages of the evolution from the material and the vital man to the mental man.

A small minority has pushed beyond the barriers, opening the doors to occult and spiritual knowledge and preparing the ascent of the evolution beyond mental man into spiritual and supramental being. Sometimes this minority has exercised an enormous influence as in Vedic India, Egypt or, according to tradition, in Atlantis, and determined the civilisation of the race, giving it a strong stamp of the spiritual or the occult; sometimes they have stood apart in their secret schools or orders, not directly influencing a civilisation which was sunk in material ignorance or in chaos and darkness or in the hard external enlightenment which rejects spiritual knowledge.

The cycles of evolution tend always upward, but they are cycles and do not ascend in a straight line. The process therefore gives the impression of a series of ascents and descents, but what is essential in the gains of the evolution is kept or, even if eclipsed for a time, reemerges in new forms suitable to the new ages.

Nut, the sky-goddess, arching to form the vault of the sky.
Ceiling of the tomb of Ramesses VI, Valley of the Kings

The Creation has descended all the degrees of being from the Supermind to Matter and in each degree it has created a world, reign, plane or order proper to that degree. In the creating of the material world there was a plunge of this descending Consciousness into an apparent Inconscience and an emergence of it out of that Inconscience, degree by degree, until it recovers its own highest spiritual and supramental summits and manifests their powers here in Matter.

But even in the Inconscience there is a secret Consciousness which works, one may say, by an involved and hidden Intuition proper to itself. In each stage of Matter, in each stage of Life, this Intuition assumes a working proper to that stage and acts from behind the veil, supporting and enforcing the immediate necessities of the creative Force.

There is an intuition in Matter which holds the action of the material Energy together and dictates the organisation of the material world from the electron to the sun and planet and their contents. There is an intuition in Life which similarly supports and guides the play and development of life in matter till it is ready for the mental evolution of which man is the vehicle.

In man also the creation follows the same upward process, – the intuition within develops according to the stage he has reached in his progress. Even the precise intellect of the scientist, who is inclined to deny the separate existence or the superiority of intuition, yet cannot really move forward unless there is behind him a mental intuition which enables him to take a forward step or to divine what has to be done. Intuition therefore is present at the beginning of things and in their middle as well as at their consummation.

But Intuition takes its proper form only when one goes beyond the mental into the spiritual domain, for there only it comes fully forward from behind the veil and reveals its true and complete nature. Along with the mental evolution of man there has been going forward the early process of another evolution which prepares the spiritual and supramental being. This has had two lines, one the discovery of the occult forces secret in Nature and of the hidden planes and worlds concealed from us by the world of Matter, and the other the discovery of man's soul and spiritual self.

If the tradition of Atlantis is correct, it is that of a progress which went to the extreme of occult knowledge but could go no farther.

In the India of Vedic times we have the record left of the other line of achievement, that of spiritual self-discovery; occult knowledge was there but kept subordinate. We may say that here in India the reign of Intuition came first, intellectual Mind developing afterwards in the later philosophy and science.

But in fact the mass of men at the time, it is quite evident, lived entirely on the material plane, worshipped the Godheads of material nature, sought from them entirely material objects.

The effort of the Vedic mystics revealed to them the things behind through a power of inner sight and hearing and experience which was confined to a limited number of seers and sages and kept carefully secret from the mass of humanity – secrecy was always insisted on by the mystics. We may very well attribute this flowering of intuition on the spiritual plane to a rapid reemergence of the essential gains brought down from a previous cycle. If we analyse the spiritual history of India we shall find that after reaching this height there was a descent which attempted to take up each lower degree of the already evolved consciousness and link it to the spiritual at the summit.

The Vedic age was followed by a great outburst of intellectual philosophy which yet took spiritual truth as its basis and tried to reach it anew, not through a direct intuitive or occult process as did the Vedic seers, but by the power of the mind's reflective, speculative, logical thought; at the same time processes of Yoga were developed which used the thinking mind as a means of arriving at spiritual realisation, spiritualising this mind itself at the same time. Then followed an era of the development of philosophies and Yoga processes which more and more used the emotional and aesthetic being as the means of spiritual realisation and spiritualised the emotional level in man through the heart and feeling. This was accompanied by Tantric and other processes which took up the mental will, the life-will, the life of sensations and made them at once the instruments and the field of spiritualisation.

In Hatha Yoga and in the various attempts at divinisation of the body there is also a line of endeavour which attempted to arrive at the same achievement with regard to living matter; but this still awaits the discovery of the true characteristic method and power of spirit in the body.

We may say therefore that the universal Consciousness after its descent into Matter has conducted the evolution there along two lines, one of ascent to the discovery of the self and spirit, the other of descent through the already evolved levels of mind, life and body so as to bring down the spiritual consciousness into these also and to fulfil thereby some secret intention in the creation of the material universe.

Our Yoga is in its principle a taking up and summarising and completing of this process, an endeavour to rise to the highest possible supramental level and bring down its consciousness and powers into mind, life and body.

The condition of present-day civilisation, materialistic with an externalised intellect and life-endeavour, which you find so painful, is an episode, but one which was perhaps inevitable. For if the spiritualisation of mind, life and body is the thing to be achieved, the conscious presence of the Spirit even in the physical consciousness and material body, an age which puts Matter and the physical life in the forefront and devotes itself to the effort of the intellect to discover the truth of material existence, had perhaps to come.

On one side, by materialising everything up to intellect itself it has created the extreme difficulty of which you speak for the spiritual seeker; but on the other hand it has given the life in Matter an importance which the spirituality of the past was inclined to deny to it.

In a way it has made the spiritualisation of it a necessity for spiritual seeking and so aided the descent movement of the evolving spiritual Consciousness in the earth-nature.

More than that we cannot claim for it; its conscious effect has been rather to stifle and almost extinguish the spiritual element in humanity; it is only by the divine use of the pressure of contraries and an intervention from above that there will be the greater spiritual outcome.

Sri Aurobindo, Letters on Yoga
Spiritual Evolution and the Supramental

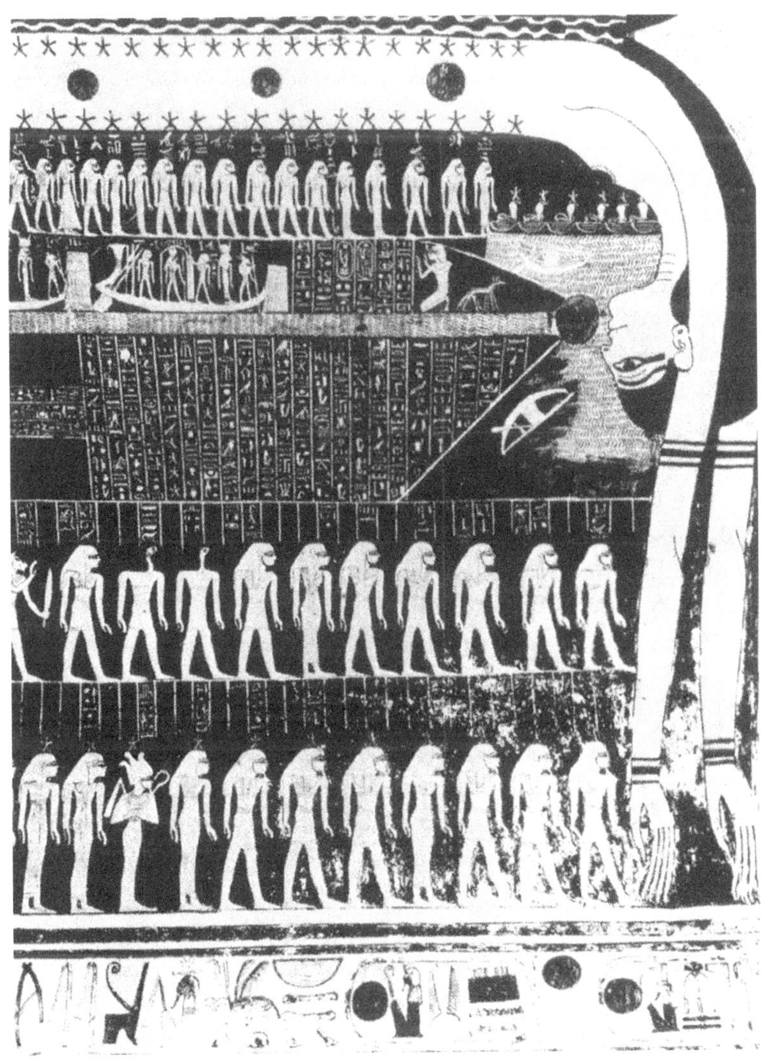

Nut, the sky-goddess, arching to form the vault of the sky.
Ceiling of the tomb of Ramesses VI, Valley of the Kings

Nature - The World-Manifestation

God is not a Being who creates & governs the universe, but the universe itself & all besides that is Timeless, & Spaceless.

God is also a Being who creates the universe in Himself & governs it; for the universe is only one term of His existence. If one could conceive a centre that contains its own circle, we might have a just definition of God in the universe.

What is the Impersonality of God? It is the fact of the Is Not, the Is & the Becoming. And what is the personality of God? It is the fact that all this, the Is like the Becoming, the Is not like the Is, is aware of itself in Time & Space & beyond them.

The Impersonality of Love is a self-existent Delight which embraces, possesses & makes one in being all that manifests in Brahman. The Personality of Love is One who is aware of self-Delight & extends His Love in all creatures.

Personality & Impersonality are the same reality differently conceived by Knowledge. Ego is the consciousness of the One Infinite Personality reflected in a limiting form of consciousness & distorted by the limitation. The form itself is a face of the All which has forgotten in the succession of Time moments, in the coherence of Space-units all that is behind itself & involved in itself. Ego is a bridge by which it awakes to self-Ignorance & returns towards self-Knowledge.

If we stand on the bridge facing the world of Forms we tend towards the Relative; if we face away from them we tend towards the Absolute. It is only when we have crossed the bridge that we can easily & perfectly embrace the Relative in the Absolute.

Spirit & Matter, Pure Being & Being formally extended in Space are the two poles of the universe. In Spirit there is no ego;

in substance of Matter there is no ego. In each pole ego loses itself, but in Spirit through synthesis, in Matter through dissolution.

Substance of matter, life & mind are the material which Ego uses to develop its conscious existence; there are higher infinite affirmations in which it fulfils its conscious existence.

There is a unity of essence & a unity of sum. The latter is only a synthetic formula & affirmation of multiplicity. The unity of essence is the true unity.

Unity & multiplicity are necessary to each other & one reality. Multiplicity is unity extended in its possibility; unity is multiplicity self-gathered into its essence.

Sri Aurobindo, Essays Divine and Human, pp. 149-153

॥ पृथभौमरेयाः ख्खवर्गेचत्रं ॥

The Lost Sun and the Lost Cows

"The gods who increase by our obeisance and were of old, without blame, they for man beset (by the powers of darkness) made the Dawn to shine by the Sun."

This is the finding of the Sun that was dwelling in the darkness by the Angirases through their ten months' sacrifice. Whatever may have been the origin of the image or legend, it is an old one and widespread and it supposes a long obscuration of the Sun during which man was beset by darkness.

We find it not only among the Aryans of India, but among the Mayas of America whose civilisation was a ruder and perhaps earlier type of the Egyptian culture; there too it is the same legend of the Sun concealed for many months in the darkness and recovered by the hymns and prayers of the wise men (the Angiras Rishis?).

In the Veda the recovery of the Light is first effected by the Angirases, the seven sages, the ancient human fathers, and is then constantly repeated in human experience by their agency.

It will appear from this analysis that the legend of the lost Sun and its recovery by sacrifice and by the *mantra* and the legend of the lost Cows and their recovery, also by the mantra, both carried out by Indra and the Angirases, are not two different myths, they are one. We have already asserted this identity while discussing the relations of the Cows and the Dawn.

The Cows are the rays of the Dawn, the herds of the Sun and not physical cattle. The lost Cows are the lost rays of the Sun; their recovery is the forerunner of the recovery of the lost sun. But it is now necessary to put this identity beyond all possible doubt by the clear statement of the Veda itself. ...

Therefore it is established beyond question that the cows of the Veda, the cows of the Panis, the cows which are stolen, fought for, pursued, recovered, the cows which are desired by the Rishis, the cows which are won by the hymn and the sacrifice, by the blazing fire and the god-increasing verse and the god intoxicating Soma, are symbolic cows, are the cows of Light, are, in the other and inner Vedic sense of the words go, *usrā, usriyā*, the shining ones, the radiances, the herds of the Sun, the luminous forms of the Dawn.

By this inevitable conclusion the corner-stone of Vedic interpretation is securely founded far above the gross materialism of a barbarous worship and the Veda reveals itself as a symbolic scripture, a sacred allegory whether of Sun-worship and Dawn-worship or of the cult of a higher and inner Light, of the true Sun, *satyaṁsūryam*, that dwells concealed in the darkness of our ignorance, hidden as the child of the Bird, the divine Hansa, in the infinite rock of this material existence, anante antar aśmani...

Sri Aurobindo, The Secret of the Veda, SABCL, Vol. 10

Surya Savitri, Creator and Increaser

But who, then, is Surya, the Sun, from whom these rays proceed?

He is the Master of Truth, Surya the Illuminator, Savitri the Creator, Pushan the Increaser.

His rays in their own nature are supramental activities of revelation, inspiration, intuition, luminous discernment, and they constitute the action of that transcendent principle which the Vedanta calls Vijnana, the perfect knowledge, the Veda Ritam, the Truth.

But these rays descend also into the human mentality and form at its summit the world of luminous intelligence, Swar, of which Indra is the lord.

Sri Aurobindo, Secret of the Veda, Rig-veda, SABCL, Vol. 10

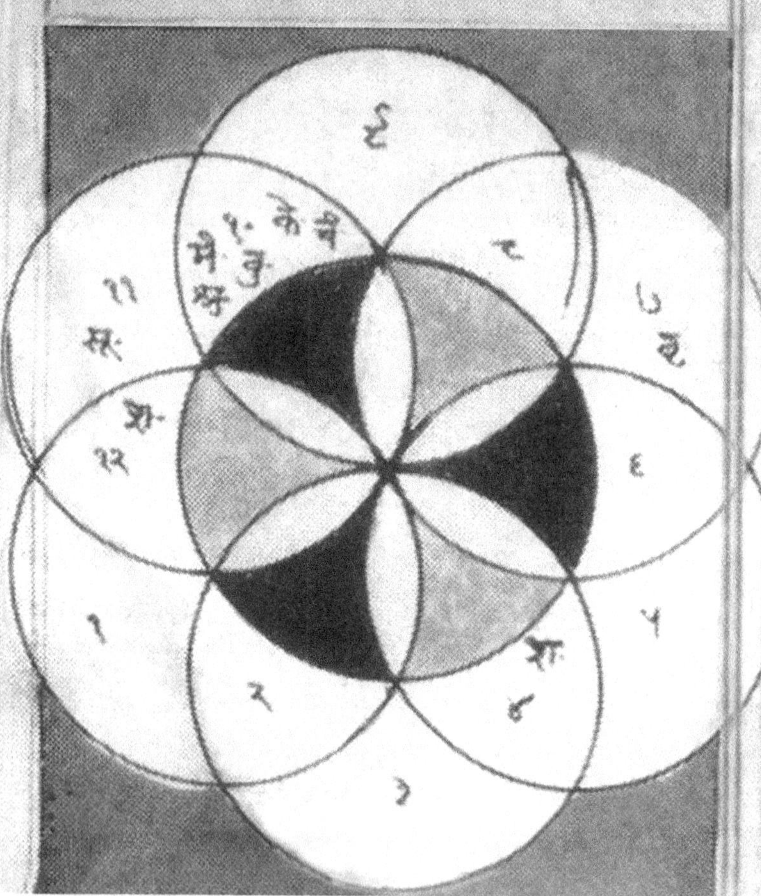

पराक्रमनाचचक्र

A Hymn to Savitri

The Rishi hymns the Sun-God as the source of divine knowledge and the creator of the inner worlds. To him, the Seer, the seekers of light yoke their mind and thoughts; he, the one knower of all forms of knowledge, is the one supreme ordainer of the sacrifice.

He assumes all forms as the robes of his being and his creative sight and creates the supreme good and happiness for the two forms of life in the worlds.

He manifests the heavenly world, shining in the path of the dawn of divine knowledge; in that path the other godheads follow him and it is his greatness of light that they make the goal of all their energies.

He has measured out for us our earthly worlds by his power and greatness: but it is in the three worlds of light that he attains to his real greatness of manifestation in the rays of the divine sun; then he encompasses the night of our darkness with his being and his light and becomes Mitra who by his laws produces the luminous harmony of our higher and lower worlds.

Of all our creation he is the one author, and by his forward marches he is its increaser until the whole world of our becoming grows full of his illumination.

Sri Aurobindo, The Secret of the Veda, SABCL, Vol. 10

The Secret below the Surface

All life, all existence is an enigma to the human mind, because the mind is a light which sees only the surfaces of things or at most a little below the surface and is moreover limited by its own circumscribed area of vision.

It cannot see what is beyond those limits and yet there are an infinity of things beyond its circle. It cannot see what is above, it cannot see what is within, it cannot see what is below. But what is on the surface is never the truth of things; the surface presents us only with facts not with truths, with phenomena not with realities, with imperfect indications, not with the realisation of things in themselves.

The secret, the truth, the reality of things is above, within, below, it is not on their surface.

✳

There is a meaning in the universe, an intention in cosmic existence; there is a significance of the individual, his life is a sign and has a purpose.

The true truth of things is not apparent on the surface, it is something hidden.

Truth is not obvious, it comes always as a discovery, Life is the working out of a secret, the process and progress of a mystery; we too are not what we seem to be, we have to find and become ourself.

What we seem to be is a thinking human animal.

What we are and have to become is God; the secret purpose of our existence here is to find the occult Reality of ourselves and the world, to become Divine.

॥ अथ बिंदु रेखा: कवर्ग चक्रम ॥

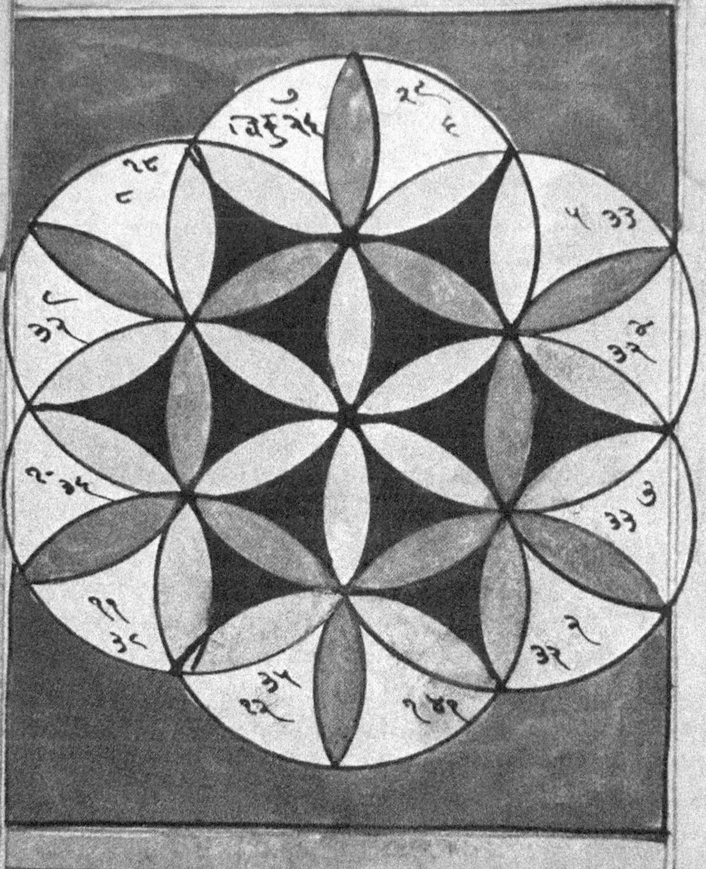

Our existence in the world has a reality which is other than that which strikes our mind and senses on the surface. It contains a secret, a mystery which we have to discover, for through that discovery we must move both to the realisation of our self and spirit and the perfection and fulfilment of our life in Nature.

Our life is not an illusion nor a delirium nor is Nature a Maya, a fabricator of dreams or a dealer in vanities as certain religions would have it nor is one the outcome of a blind Force or the trick [off a blind self-regulating Chance], the other an unconscious Power, as they must be if the materialists' dogma were true. Our life is neither a freak of God nor a freak of Nature; it has a conscious plan although a secret plan, a significance although an occult and mystic significance.

The plan, the significance, are secret and mysterious to us because we live on the surface of ourselves and things and are not in touch with either their core or their height or depths. Science on one side, Religion and Philosophy on the other try to arrive at the hidden Truth, but each touches and only just touches one end of it and refuses to go farther and discover the other end or the link and reconciling relation between these two poles of existence.

It is said in the Veda of Agni, the flame of the creative Will and Force, that he hides his two extremities; only his middle is patent and visible. The head of Agni is occult in some superconscient height, his feet are plunged in the abyss of the material Inconscience. Consciousness emerging in the universe of life and mind is the bridge and link between the two poles. But our human consciousness is a term in the chain which is aware only of itself and sees all the rest in its own terms; it cannot identify itself with the other links and misses their significance and their purpose. It stands on the middle of the bridge looking all around it, but the bridgeheads are to its sight invisible. It cannot see what is there but only speculate, infer or conjecture.

Science questing with its measuring rod of empirical experiment begins to have a dark glimpse of the Inconscient; it knows the universe as an organised freak that has emerged from the material Inconscience and will go back to its source.

Religion and Philosophy rise on the wings of spiritual experience or in a balloon of metaphysical logic into some stratosphere of superconscient Reality, they seem to discover a God or Self or Spirit or Absolute and try to map it with the intellect or to turn it into a dynamic spiritual formula. But they are unable to reconcile these three terms of being; their physical experiments or their spiritual experiences are valid, but each has hold of only one end of the enigma.

Science has discovered Evolution; Religion and Philosophy have discovered something of that which is involved and evolves in this cosmic Existence. But the two discoveries have refused to shed light upon each other; each has shut itself up in its own formulas. This is because each is a creation and activity of Mind, Science of the concretising experimental mind, philosophy of the abstracting intellectual mind, Religion of the dynamic spiritual mind. But Mind is bound always by its partial formulations of the Truth;

Mind grasps formulas or images but is itself grasped by its own creations, it cannot get free from them or go beyond them. But the mind's concepts and formulas are only fragmentary representations of Truth or pointers or abstract schemas and images, not her very self and reality. Either a deeper inner soul-vision or a higher overmental or supra-mental consciousness is needed to discover Truth in her very face and body.

The Divine entity shown as a jackal, Anubis, is charged with the
embalmment of the royal mummy, vally of the Kings

Then only can both ends of the riddle be firmly seized and connected together, the whole of existence seen in one gaze and life compelled to unmask its fathomless significance.

*

A mysterious something involved in Matter, concealed by it, evolving from it but in a material house or figure, striving to reveal itself in life and mind, but concealed by its forms of life, concealed by its forms of mind, shooting out from them glimpses of itself, glimpses that hint but do not elucidate, - this is what we can see, and we see no more; the rest is speculation and conjecture.

Is this something native to Matter, born in it and destined to die in it?

Or is it an alien, a temporary visitor? Is Matter itself only a mask of it, a phenomenon of Energy, as it now more and more seems to be? Energy itself is a movement, a force of concealed Consciousness, Consciousness the sign of a hidden spiritual Being. But if so, what possible significance or purpose can there be in this involution, this material self-concealment and self-imprisonment, this slow tormented emergence of the Spirit?

Two lines of enquiry seem to give, though imperfectly and in opposition, a positive base for a reply to the question and the riddle, - the experiments of the scientist and the experience of the mystic.

Sri Aurobindo, Essays Divine and Human, 90, 91, 92, pp. 301-384

The Sun

The sun is the symbol of the concentrated light of Truth.

✸

The Sun is the Truth-Light of the One Existence and the flame the dynamic power of action (Yogic) of that Truth-Light.

✸

The Sun is the divine Truth-Light on whatever plane of consciousness. It is, I suppose, the original cosmic Truth that is here indicated.

✸

The Sun is the Truth from above, in the last resort the Supramental Truth.

✸

The sun is the symbol of the Supermind.

✸

The sun rising on the horizon is the direct light of the Divine Truth rising in the being—the ray upwards opens the being to the Truth as it is above mind, the ray in front opens it to what we call the cosmic consciousness, it becomes released from the personal limitation and opens and becomes aware of the universal mind, universal physical, universal vital. The action on the heart was the pressure of this Sun on it to have this direct opening, so that the consciousness may become free, wide and wholly at peace.

✸

There are different suns in the different planes, each with its own colour. But there are also suns of a similar colour above, only more bright, from which these minor suns derive their light and power.

*

The golden [Sun] is the Light of the Truth on the higher planes. The white [Sun] is the Sun of the Mother's consciousness (the Divine Consciousness) which manifests on all the planes.

*

The white sun indicates the purity and peace of the Divine Consciousness.

*

The red sun is a symbol of the true, illumined physical consciousness which is to replace the obscure and ignorant physical consciousness in which men now live. Red is the colour of the physical; the red diamond is the Mother's consciousness in the physical.

*

In the experience the disc of the sun indicates the supramental consciousness with the Divine Being in it (the supramental Divine who can bridge by his light the gulf between the higher and the lower consciousness and unify them). But the smoky appearance, the veil etc. indicated that there was something in the (human) nature that made rapid realisation difficult. This was what was also said by the voice that the time was not yet. Obviously the supramental cannot be achieved except by a long sadhana—the experience should not be taken as meaning anything more than that.

Sri Aurobindo, The Secret of the Veda, Letters on Yoga - III, Book III

Man and the Supermind

The disk of a secret sun of Power and Joy and Knowledge is emerging...

Man is a transitional being, he is not final; for in him and high beyond him ascend the radiant degrees which climb to a divine supermanhood.

The step from man towards superman is the next approaching achievement in the earth's evolution. There lies our destiny and the liberating key to our aspiring, but troubled and limited human existence — inevitable because it is at once the intention of the inner Spirit and the logic of Nature's process.

The appearance of a human possibility in a material and animal world was the first glint of a coming divine Light, — the first far-off intimation of a godhead to be born out of Matter. The appearance of the superman in the human world will be the fulfilment of that distant shining promise.

The difference between man and superman will be the difference between mind and a consciousness as far beyond it as thinking mind is beyond the consciousness of plant and animal; the differentiating essence of man is mind, the differentiating essence of superman will be supermind or a divine gnosis.

Man is a mind imprisoned, obscured and circumscribed in a precarious and imperfect living but imperfectly conscious body. The superman will be a supramental spirit which will envelop and freely use a conscious body, plastic to spiritual forces. His physical frame will be a firm support and an adequate radiant instrument for the spirit's divine play and work in Matter.

Mind, even free and in its own unmixed and unhampered element, is not the highest possibility of consciousness; for mind is not in possession of Truth, but only a minor vessel or an instrument and here an ignorant seeker plucking eagerly at a mass of falsehoods and half-truths for the unsatisfying pabulum of its hunger. Beyond mind is a supramental or gnostic power of consciousness that is in eternal possession of Truth; all its motion and feeling and sense and outcome are instinct and luminous with the inmost reality of things and express nothing else.

Supermind or gnosis is in its original nature at once and in the same movement an infinite wisdom and an infinite will. At its source it is the dynamic consciousness of the divine Knower and Creator.

When in the process of unfolding of an always greater force of the one Existence, some delegation of this power shall descend into our limited human nature, then and then only can man exceed himself and know divinely and divinely act and create; he will have become at last a conscious portion of the Eternal. The superman will be born, not a magnified mental being, but a supramental power descended here into a new life of the transformed terrestrial body. A gnostic supermanhood is the next distinct and triumphant victory to be won by the spirit descended into earthly nature.

The disk of a secret sun of Power and Joy and Knowledge is emerging out of the material consciousness in which our mind works as a chained slave or a baffled and impotent demiurge; supermind will be the formed body of that radiant effulgence.

Superman is not man climbed to his own natural zenith, not a superior degree of human greatness, knowledge, power, intelligence, will, character, genius, dynamic force, saintliness, love, purity or perfection. Supermind is something beyond mental man and his limits, a greater consciousness than the highest consciousness proper to human nature.

Man is a being from the mental worlds whose mentality works here involved, obscure and degraded in a physical brain, shut off from its own divinest powers and impotent to change life beyond certain narrow and precarious limits. Even in the highest of his kind it is baulked of its luminous possibilities of supreme force and freedom by this dependence. Most often and in most men it is only a servitor, a purveyor of amusements, a caterer of needs and interests to the life and the body. But the superman will be a gnostic king of Nature; supermind in him even in its evolutionary beginnings will appear as a ray of the eternal omniscience and omnipotence. Sovereign and irresistible it will lay hands on the mental and physical instruments, and, standing above and yet penetrating and possessing our lower already manifested parts, it will transform mind, life and body into its own divine and luminous nature.

Man in himself is hardly better than an ambitious nothing. He is a narrowness that reaches towards ungrasped widenesses, a littleness straining towards grandeurs which are beyond him, a dwarf enamoured of the heights. His mind is a darkened ray in the splendours of the universal Mind. His life is a striving exulting and suffering wave, an eager passion-tossed and sorrow-stricken or a blindly and dully toiling petty moment of the universal Life. His body is a labouring perishable speck in the material universe. An immortal soul is somewhere hidden within him and gives out from time to time some sparks of its presence, and an eternal spirit is above and overshadows with its wings and upholds with its power this soul continuity in his nature. But that greater spirit is obstructed from descent by the hard lid of his constructed personality and this inner radiant soul is wrapped, stifled and oppressed in dense outer coatings. In all but a few it is seldom active, in many hardly perceptible. The soul and spirit in man seem rather to exist above and behind his formed nature than to be a part of its visible reality; subliminal in his inner being or superconscient above in some unreached status, they are in his outer consciousness possibilities rather than things realised and present. The spirit is in course of birth rather than born in Matter.

This imperfect being with his hampered, confused, ill-ordered and mostly ineffective consciousness cannot be the end and highest height of the mysterious upward surge of Nature. There is something more that has yet to be brought down from above and is now seen only by broken glimpses through sudden rifts in the giant wall of our limitations. Or else there is something yet to be evolved from below, sleeping under the veil of man's mental consciousness or half visible by flashes, as life once slept in the stone and metal, mind in the plant and reason in the cave of animal memory underlying its imperfect apparatus of emotion and sense-device and instinct. Something there is in us yet unexpressed that has to be delivered by an enveloping illumination from above. A godhead is imprisoned in our depths, one in its being with a greater godhead ready to descend from superhuman summits. In that descent and awakened joining is the secret of our future.

Man's greatness is not in what he is but in what he makes possible. His glory is that he is the closed place and secret workshop of a living labour in which supermanhood is made ready by a divine Craftsman.

But he is admitted to a yet greater greatness and it is this that, unlike the lower creation, he is allowed to be partly the conscious artisan of his divine change. His free assent, his consecrated will and participation are needed that into his body may descend the glory that will replace him. His aspiration is earth's call to the supramental Creator.

If earth calls and the Supreme answers, the hour can be even now for that immense and glorious transformation.

Sri Aurobindo, Essays Divine and Human

The Supreme Mahashakti

The secret name of the Supreme Mahashakti signifies

मयोभूः . . राधा	Love, Bliss,	**Ananda**
महामाया, पराप्रकृति	Creative and Formative Knowledge - Power	**Chit-Tapas**
	Support, Covering, Pervasion	**Sat**

For the Supreme is Ananda unifying Consciousness and Existence in the single Power (Shakti) of these things.

✸

All is created by the Supreme Goddess, the *Supreme and Original Mahashakti,* all proceeds from her, all lives by her, all lives in her, even as she lives in all. All wisdom and knowledge are her wisdom and knowledge; all power is her power, all will and force her will and force, all action is her action, all movement her movement. All beings are portions of her power of existence.

Seven times seven are the planes of the Supreme Goddess, the steps of ascent and descent of the Divine Transcendent and Universal Adyashakti.

Above are the thrice seven supreme planes of Sat-Chit-Ananda; तूरः सप्त परमा पदानिमातुः; in between are the seven planes of the Divine Truth and Vastness, Mahad Brahma; सत्यमृतं बृहत्; below are the thrice seven steps of the ascent and descent into this evolutionary world of the earth existence.

These three gradations are successively Supermind or Truth-Mind, with its seven suns; Life with its seven Lotuses; Earth with its seven Jewel-Centres.

The seven Lotuses are the seven chakras of the Tantric tradition, descending and ascending from Mind (Sahasradala, Ajna, Vishuddha, Anahata) that takes up Life through Life in Force (Manipura, Swadhisthana) down to Life involved in Matter (Mūlādhāra).

All these Life-Centres are in themselves centres of Truth in Life even as the seven Suns are each a flaming heart of Truth in luminous Divine-Mind-Existence; but these lotuses have been veiled, closed, shut into their own occult energies by the Ignorance. Hence the obscurity, falsehood, death, suffering of our existence.

The Jewel-Centres of the Earth-Mother are seven luminous jewel-hearts of Truth in Substance, but they have been imprisoned in darkness, fossilised in immobility, veiled, closed, shut into their own occult energies by the hardness, darkness and inertia of the material Inconscience.

To liberate all these powers by the luminous and flaming descent of the suns of the Supermind and the release of the eighth Sun of Truth hidden in the Earth, in the darkness of the Inconscience, in the cavern of Vala and his Panis, this is the first step towards the restoration of the Earth Mother to her own divinity and the earth-existence to its native light, truth, life and bliss of immaculate Ananda.

Sri Aurobindo, Record of Yoga, Vol. 10, The Hour of God,
The Absolute and the Manifestation

Earth Grid / Earth Matrix

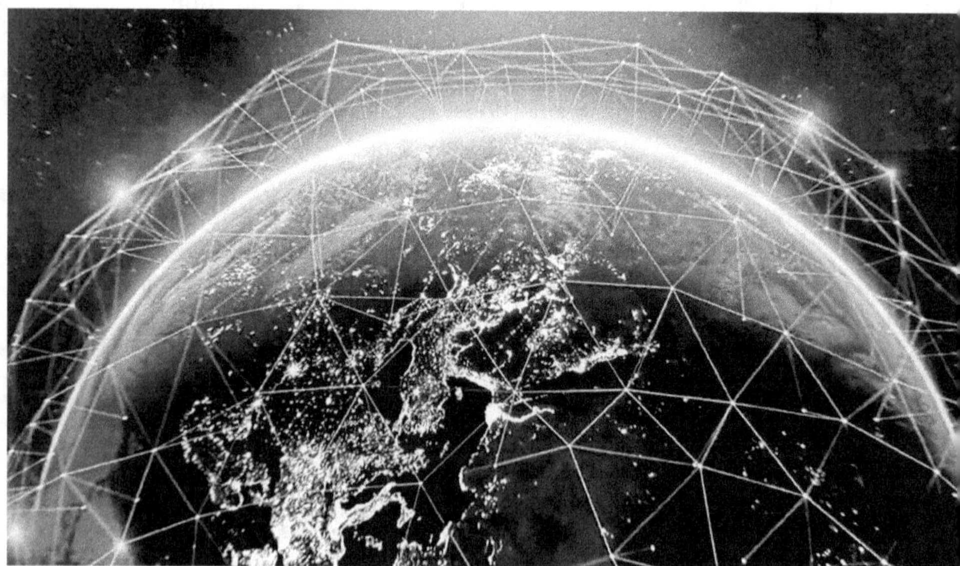

The Seven Suns of the Supermind

1. The Sun of Supramental Truth, — Knowledge-Power originating the supramental creation.

    Descent into the Sahasradala.

2. The Sun of Supramental Light and Will-Power, transmitting the Knowledge Power as dynamic vision and command to create, found and organise the supramental creation.

    Descent into the Ajna-chakra, the centre between the eyes.

3. The Sun of the Supramental Word, embodying the Knowledge-Power, empowered to express and arrange the supramental creation.

    Descent into the Throat-Centre.

4. The Sun of supramental Love, Beauty and Bliss, releasing the Soul of the Knowledge-Power to vivify and harmonise the supramental creation.

    Descent into the Heart-Lotus

5. The Sun of Supramental Force dynamised as a power and source of life to support the supramental creation Descent into the navel centre

6. The Sun of Life-Radiances (Power-Rays) distributing the dynamis and pouring it into concrete formations.

    Descent into the penultimate centre

7. The Sun of supramental Substance-Energy and Form-Energy empowered to embody the supramental life and stabilise the creation.

    Descent into the Mūlādhāra.

Sri Aurobindo

The Hour of God, Section III, The Absolute and the Manifestation
(Record of Yoga, Vol. 10)

Earth Chakras and Sacred Sites

The Jewel-Centres of the Earth-Mother
are seven luminous jewel-hearts of Truth in Substance...

(Geo-Spiritual Mapping by Michael Miovic)

Chakra	Plane of Consciousness	Jewel Centre
1. Sahasradala	Intuitive Planes (Several Levels)	Maha-Asia
2. Ajna	Mental Proper (Reason, Ideas, Will)	Maha-Europa
3. Visuddha	Externalizing Mind (Power, Action)	Maha-Asiatica Minoris
4. Anahata	Higher Vital (Heart, Emotion)	Maha-Africa
5. Manipura	Central Vital (Major Life Motives)	Maha-Pacifica (Middle)
6. Svadisthana	Lower Vital (Creative Energies)	Maha-Pacifica (South)
7. Muladhara	Physical Proper (Substance, Matter)	Maha-America
(Subconscient)	Subconscious Memory and Habits	Maha-Australia
(Inconscient)	Existential Void or Darkness	Maha-Antarctica

The Seven Earth Chakras and Sacred Sites

Energy Grid System

When mapped-out, the invisible lines that connect these sacred sites and many major cities around the world are commonly called "Ley Lines" by the Western scientists, archaeologists, quantum physicists and mystics who have studied them. In China they are referred to as "Dragon Lines" and in South America "Spirit Lines".

The two main lines are also sometimes called the "Serpent Ley Lines" which represent divine feminine and masculine energies and intertwine to form an infinity symbol. These veins of subtle energy create the grid system that transmits frequencies throughout the entire planet — very similar to the energetic network and inner workings of our own human electromagnetic field, meridians and circulatory system.

Earth Chakras, Harwitum Australia, Ater Tumti, Matias de Stefano

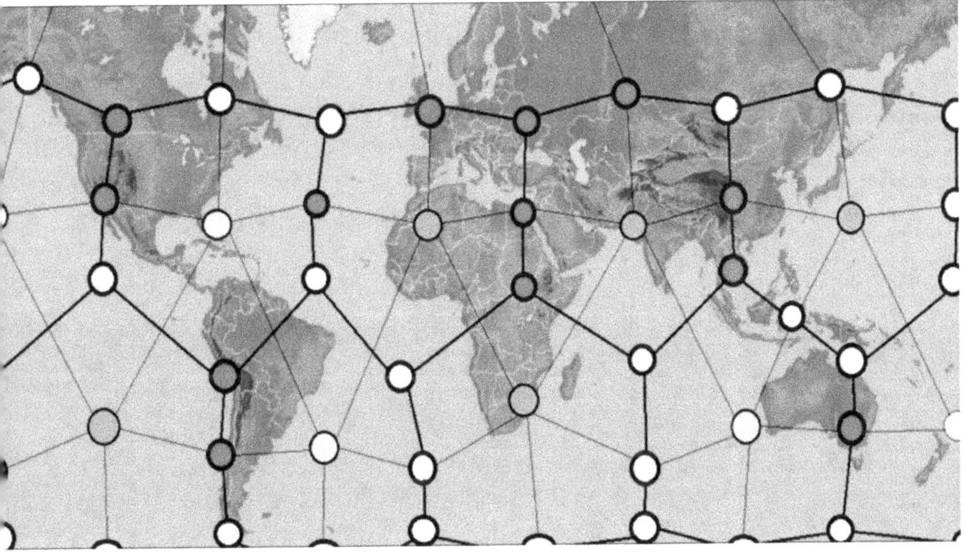

The Seven Centres of the Life

1. The thousand-petalled Lotus — above the head with its base on the brain. Basis or support in Life-Mind for the Supramental; initiative centre of the illumined Mind.

2. The centre between the brows in the middle of the forehead. Will, vision, inner mental formation, active and dynamic Mind.

3. The centre in the throat. Speech, external mind, all external expression and formation.

4. The heart-lotus. Externally, the emotional mind, the vital mental: in the inner heart the psychic centre.

5. The navel centre. The larger vital proper; life-force centre.

6. The centre intermediate between the navel and the Mūlādhāra. The lower vital; it connects all the above centres with the physical.

7. The last centre or Mūlādhāra. Material support of the vital; initiation of the physical.

All below is the subconscient physical.

Sri Aurobindo
The Hour of God, Section III, The Absolute and the Manifestation, p.87
(Record of Yoga, Vol. 10)

The meridians in our physical, emotional, spiritual and energetic bodies are mirrors of the meridians and ley lines that span across the planet earth, the greater universe and cosmic atmosphere.

Gayatri mantra personified as a goddess

Gayatri Mantra

The **Gāyatrī Mantra** (Sanskrit: गायत्री मन्त्र), also known as the **Sāvitri Mantra** (Sanskrit: सावित्री मन्त्र), is a highly revered mantra from the *Rig Veda* (Mandala 3.62.10), dedicated to the Vedic deity Savitr. *Gāyatri* is the name of the Goddess of the Vedic meter in which the verse is composed. Its recitation is traditionally preceded by *om* and the formula *bhūr bhuvah svah*, known as the *mahāvyāhrti*, or "great (mystical) utterance". The Gayatri mantra is cited widely in Hindu texts, such as the mantra listings of the Śrauta liturgy, and classical Hindu texts such as the *Bhagavad Gita*, *Harivamsa*, and *Manusmrti*. The mantra and its associated metric form was known by the Buddha. The mantra is an important part of the upanayana ceremony. Modern Hindu reform movements spread the practice of the mantra to everyone and its use is now very widespread.

ॐ भूर्भुव स्सुवः
तत्स॑ वितुर्वरे॑ ण्यं
भर्गो॑ देवस्य॑ धीमहि
धियो॑ यो नः॑ प्रचो॑दयात् ॥

**Om bhūr bhuvah suvah
tat savitur varenyam
bhargo devasya dhīmahi
dhiyo yo nah pracodayāt**

– Rigveda 3.62.10

The main mantra appears in the hymn RV 3.62.10. During its recitation, the hymn is preceded by oṃ (ॐ) and the formula bhūr bhuvaḥ svaḥ (भूर् भुवः स्वः). This prefixing of the mantra is properly described in the Taittiriya Aranyaka (2.11.1-8), which states that it should be chanted with the syllable oṃ, followed by the three Vyahrtis and the Gayatri verse. Whereas in principle the gāyatrī mantra specifies three pādas of eight syllables each, the text of the verse as preserved in the Samhita is one short, seven instead of eight. Metrical restoration would emend the attested tri-syllabic varenyam with a tetra-syllabic vareniyam.

Dedication

The *Gāyatrī* mantra is dedicated to Savitṛi, a Sun deity. The mantra is attributed to the much revered sage Vishwamitra, who is also considered the author of Mandala 3 of Rig Veda. Many monotheistic sects of Hinduism such as Arya Samaj hold that the Gayatri mantra is in praise of One Supreme Creator known by the name Om as mentioned in the *Yajur Veda*, 40:17.

Swami Vivekananda

"We meditate on the glory of that Being who has produced this universe; may She enlighten our minds."

Sri Aurobindo

"We choose the Supreme Light of the divine Sun; we aspire that it may impel our minds." Sri Aurobindo further elaborates: "The Sun is the symbol of divine Light that is coming down and Gayatri gives expression to the aspiration asking that divine Light to come down and give impulsion to all the activities of the mind."

Literal translations of the Gāyatrī Mantra

Om - Para Brahman (entire universe);

Bhur - Bhuloka (physical plane);

Bhuvah - Antariksha (space);

Suvah - Svarga Loka (Heaven);

Tat - Paramatma (Supreme Soul);

Savitur - Isvara (Surya) (Sun god);

Varenyam - Fit to be worshipped;

Bhargo - Remover of sins and ignorance;

Devasya - Glory (Jnana Svaroopa i.e. Feminine / Female);

Dheemahi - We meditate;

Dhiyo - Buddhi (Intellect);

Yo - Which;

Nah - Our;

Prachodayat: Enlighten / inspire.

Sri Aurobindo's Gayatri Mantra

तत्सवितुर्वरं रूपं ज्योतिः परस्य धीमहि ।
यन्नः सत्येन दीपयेत् ॥

Tat savitur varam rūpam jyotiḥ parasya dhīmahi,
yannaḥ satyena dīpayet

Let us meditate on the most auspicious form of Savitri, on the Light of the Supreme which shall illumine us with the Truth.

Let us meditate on the most auspicious (best) form of Savitri, on the Light of the Supreme which shall illumine us with the Truth.

The Mother's Gayatri

The most sacred Mantra of the Rigveda (III.62.10), the Gayatri of Rishi Vishwamitra, directs us to the Solar Godhead of Truth -Surya-Savitri:

Tat savitur vareṇyaṁ
bhargo devasya dhīmahi
dhiyo yo naḥ prachodayat

Let us meditate
on that most excellent light
of the divine Savitri
that it may impel our minds.

It is hardly possible for the Mother to have come across this great formula of Yogic progress in Paris in 1911. But just at that time, she gave a speech to a Women's Association. It makes a study of the anatomy of thought and explains how thinking can be controlled and turned into a perfect servant. Her speech ends with the exhortation:

"I would like us to make the resolution to raise ourselves each day, in all sincerity and goodwill, in an ardent aspiration towards the Sun of Truth, towards the Supreme Light, the source and intellectual life of the universe, so that it may pervade us entirely and illumine with its great brilliance our minds and hearts, all our thoughts and our actions."

Here is indeed a spontaneous reflection of the master Mantra
- rather a recurrence of it from the same depths that it originally
surged up from. But what is even more striking is that the Mother's
version anticipates in living essence the new Gayatri which Sri
Aurobindo has been inspired to give us, crystallising the aspiration
for the direct descent of the Supermind into our earthly being:

Tat saviturvaram rūpam
jyotiḥ parasya dhīmahi
yannah satyena dīpayet

Let us meditate
on the most auspicious (best) form of Savitri,
on the Light of the Supreme
which shall illumine us with the Truth.

Amal Kiran, The Sun and The Rainbow, pp. 116-117

The Island Sun

I have sailed the golden ocean
And crossed the silver bar;
I have reached the Sun of knowledge,
The earth-self's midnight star.

Its fields of flaming vision,
Its mountains of bare might,
Its peaks of fiery rapture,
Its air of absolute light,

Its seas of self-oblivion,
Its vales of Titan rest,
Became my soul's dominion,
Its Island of the Blest.

Alone with God and silence,
Timeless it lived in Time;
Life was His fugue of music,
Thought was Truth's ardent rhyme.

The Light was still around me
When I came back to earth
Bringing the Immortal's knowledge
Into man's cave of birth.

Sri Aurobindo, 13th October 1939, CWSA, Collected Poems

The Golden Age

Part of the teaching of Pythagoras is a belief in the existence of a Golden Age. Pythagoras learned this when he was studying in Egypt, and made this teaching his own. The existence of a Golden Age was part of Egyptian culture, and a way to explain its origin.

It was said that in archaic, predynastic times - that is before the first human pharaoh of the first dynasty some 5,000 years ago - there were divine pharaohs and divine dynasties: the dynasty of PTAH, the dynasty of RE, the dynasty of OSIRIS and ISIS, the dynasty of SETH, etc. And for each of those dynasties they could say how long it lasted. The dynasty of PTAH, for example, according to a Greek list, lasted 9,000 years.

The belief that there was once a blessed golden time of joyous accomplishment is common to many ancient civilisations.

In India the Satya Yuga, the age of golden knowledge and truth, is said to belong to a cycle that repeats itself: it existed in the past and will exist again in the future.

In Egypt a golden way of being was the aim of a pharaoh's life, and could be attained by yogic psychological games and exercises. He would then become the golden HORUS.

In contrast to the school of Pythagoras, another Greek tradition, that of Democritus, stated that the life of prehistoric man was short, brutal and nasty. From this crude beginning, humanity is supposed to be developing constantly. But this constant steady progress is not obvious. How far have we advanced since the time of Democritus?

Rhythmic ups and downs are more the way of nature. Like ice ages and interglacial ages - but also because of or in spite of them - flowering plants and butterflies have come to stay.

May not every Golden Age leave behind it when it goes something like a golden deposit for future generations to dream about?

Medhananda, On the threshold of a new age with Medhananda

The Sociology of Superman

There are ten or twenty, perhaps fifty, here or there, in one latitude or another, who yearn to till a truer plot of land, a small patch of man to grow a truer being within themselves, perhaps create together a laboratory of the superman, lay the first stone of the City of Truth on earth. They do not know, they do not know anything, except that they need something else and that there exists a Law of Harmony, a marvellous "something" of the Future seeking to be incarnated. They want to find the conditions of that incarnation, to lend themselves to the trial, to offer their substance for that living experiment.

They know nothing except that everything must be different: in hearts, in gestures, in matter and the handling of matter.

They are not seeking to create a new civilization, but another man; not a supercity among the millions of buildings of the world, but a listening post for the forces of the future, a supreme yantra of Truth, a conduit, a channel to try to capture and inscribe in matter a first note of the great Harmony, a first tangible sign of the new world.

They do not pose as the champions of anything; they do not defend any liberty or attack any ism. They simply try together. They are the champions of their own pure little note, which is unlike the next person's and yet is everyone's note. They are no longer from a country, a family, a religion or a party; they belong to their own party, which is no one else's and yet is the party of the world, because what becomes true at one point becomes true for the whole world and brings the whole world together.

They are from a family to be invented, from a country yet to be born. They do not try to correct others or anybody, to pour self-glorifying charities over the world, to cure the poor and the lepers ; they try to cure the great poverty of smallness in themselves, the gray elf of the inner misery, to reclaim one single parcel of truth from themselves, one single ray of harmony. For if that Disease is cured in our own heart or a few hearts, the world will be that much lighter, and, through our clarity, the Law of Truth will better penetrate matter and radiate all around spontaneously. What liberation, what relief can a man who suffers in his own heart bring to the world?

They do not work for themselves, though they are the primary ground of the experience, but as an offering, pure and simple, to that which they do not really know, but which shimmers at the edge of the world like the dawn of a new age.

They are the prospectors of the new cycle. They have given themselves to the future, body and soul, the way one jumps into the fire, without a look back.

They are the servants of the infinite in the finite, of the totality in the infinitesimal, of eternity in each second and each gesture.

They create their heaven with each step and carve the new world out of the banality of the day. And they are not afraid of failure, for they have left behind the failures and success of the prison - they live in the sole infallibility of a right little note.

But these builders of the new world will have to be careful not to erect a new prison, be it an ideal and enlightened one. In fact, they will understand, and quickly, that this City of Truth will not and cannot see the light of day until they themselves live totally in the Truth, and that that building site is first and foremost the site of their own transmutation.

One does not deceive Truth. One may deceive men, make speeches and declarations of principle, but Truth doesn't care a damn. It catches you in the act and throws your deception right back into your face at every step. It is a merciless searchlight, even if it is invisible. And it is very simple; it catches you every time, at every twist and turn; and since it is a Truth of matter, it foils your plans, checks your gesture, confronts you with a sudden lack of materials, workers or funds, stirs up revolt, sets people at odds with each other, sows impossibilities and chaos - until, suddenly, the seeker realizes that he was on the wrong track, putting up the old false structure with new bricks and exuding his small egoism, small ambition or small ideal, his narrow idea of truth and good.

So he opens his eyes, opens his hands, attunes himself again to the great Law, lets the rhythm flow, and becomes clear, clear and transparent, plastic to the Truth, to the something seeking to be - anything as long as it be that, the exact gesture, the right thought, the true work, the pure truth expressing itself as it wishes, when it wishes, in the way it wishes. For a second he lets go of everything.

For a second he calls out to that new world - so new he understands nothing of it, but which he wants to serve, embody, grow in this rebellious soil. What does it matter what he thinks, feels or deems, oh, what difference does it really make? - just let it be the true thing, the one necessary and inevitable thing. And everything tips into the light - in a second.

Everything instantly becomes possible: the materials arrive, and the workers and the funds, the wall crumbles, and the little egoistic structure he was building changes into a dynamic possibility he had not even suspected.

He repeats this experience a hundred times, a thousand times, at every level, personal and collective, from the repair of his bedroom window to the sudden million that comes as a "godsend" to build that Olympic stadium.

There are no material problems, ever; there are only inner problems. And if Truth is not there, even the millions will rot on the spot. It is a fabulous experience every minute, a test of Truth and, even more marvellously, a test of the power of Truth. Step by step he learns to discover the effectiveness of Truth, the supreme effectiveness of a clear little second - he enters a world of continuous little marvels. He learns to trust Truth, as if all those blows, blunders, conflicts and confusion were leading him knowingly, patiently, but relentlessly to take the right attitude, to discover the true lever, the true look, the cry of truth that topples walls and makes every possibility blossom amid the impossible chaos.

It is an accelerated transmutation, multiplied by the resistance of each one as much as by the goodwill of each one - as if, truly, both resistance and goodwill, good and evil, had to be changed into something else, another will, a will-vision of Truth that decides the gesture and action at each instant.

This is the only law of the City of the Future, its only government: a clear vision that accords with the total Harmony, and spontaneously translates the perceived Truth into action. The fakers are automatically eliminated by the very pressure of the Force of Truth, driven out, like fish, by a sheer excess of oxygen. And if one day these ten or fifty could build a single little pyramid of truth, whose every stone has been laid with the right note, the right vibration, simple love, a clear look and a call to the future, the whole city would actually be built, because they would have built the being of the future in themselves.

And perhaps the whole earth would find itself changed by it, because there is only one body, because the difficulty of the one is the difficulty of the world, the resistance and darkness of the other are the resistance and darkness of the whole world, and because that insignificant little enterprise of a tiny city under the stars may be the very Enterprise of the world, the symbol of its transmutation, the alchemy of its pain, the possibility of a new earth by the single transfiguration of one piece of earth and one piece of mankind.

It is therefore probable that for a long time this City under construction will be a place where negative possibilities will be exacerbated as much as the positive ones, under the relentless pressure of the beacon of Truth. And falsehood is skilled at holding on to insignificant details, resistance at sticking to everyday trifles, which become the very sign of refusal.

Falsehood knows how to make great sacrifices. It can follow a discipline, extol an ideal, collect merit badges and Brownie points, but it betrays itself in the insignificant - that is its last refuge. It is really in matter that the game is played out.

This City of the Future is a battle-field, a difficult adventure. What is decided over there with machine guns, guerilla warfare and glorious deeds is decided here with sordid details and an invisible warfare against falsehood.

But a single victory won over petty human egoism is more pregnant with consequences for the earth than the rearranging of all the frontiers of Asia, for this frontier and this egoism are the original barbed wire that divides the world.

Satprem, On the Way to Supermanhood

Then who was the Mother?

She was the Ancient One of evolution who had come to make a new cleft in the old, tedious habit of being a man ... She was the adventuress par excellence - the adventuress of the earth. She was there to discover ... another Species ... a new Matter ... a new Spirit.

The "other species" was really radically other, and yet it was vibrating within, absolutely recognizable, as if it were THAT we had been seeking from age to age, THAT we had been invoking through all our illuminations, one after another, in Thebes as in Eleusis as everywhere we have toiled and grieved in the skin of a man. It was for THAT we were here, for that supreme Possible?[1]

From 1958 to 1975, She slowly uncovered the "Great Passage" to the next species and a new mode of life in Matter. This is the Agenda.

In 1968, she founded Auroville, a few miles outside Pondicherry, as a "laboratory of the new evolution".

Satprem

---

1 Satprem, Introduction to The Mother's Agenda
   Institut de Recherches Evolutives, Paris & Mira Aditi, Mysore

Queen Hatshepsut, at the Deir el-Bahri temple in Luxor

Queen Hatshepsut

Hatshepsut, 1507–1458 BCE, was the fifth pharaoh of the Eighteenth Dynasty of Egypt. As the principal wife of Thutmose II, Hatshepsut initially ruled as regent to Thutmose III. While Thutmose III had inherited the throne at about two years old, Hatshepsut continued to rule by asserting her lineage as the daughter and only child of Thutmose I and his primary wife, Ahmose. Hatshepsut assumed the position of pharaoh or king c. 1478 or 1479 BCE and ruled until 1458 BEC, the year of her death.

Hatshepsut's reign is well-known for increased prosperity, large-scale construction projects such as the Karnak Temple Complex, Speos Artemidos, the Mortuary Temple of Hatshepsut and Red Chapel of Hatshepsut (Chapelle Rouge). Hatshepsut and her supporters used traditional religious beliefs to enforce her role as pharaoh and king, despite these being considered men's roles.

After her death, she was not mentioned in official accounts of Egyptian historiography by her successors, possibly due to sibling rivalry, political expediency, or due to her gender.

Hatshepsut was married to Thutmose II, her half-brother, when she was 14 or 15 years old. They were around the same age when they got married.

Upon the death of Thutmose II, Thutmose III became the pharaoh of Egypt. Hatshepsut served as co-regent during his reign, and was thought of by early modern scholars as only having served as a co-regent alongside Thutmose III. However, modern scholars agree that Hatshepsut later assumed the position of pharaoh c. 1478 BCE. Although queens Sobekneferu and Nitocris may have previously assumed the roles of pharaoh, Hatshepsut was the only female ruler to do so in a time of prosperity, and had more powers than her female predecessors.

Hatshepsut was described as having a reign of about 21 years by ancient authors. Josephus and Julius Africanus both quote Manetho's king list, mentioning a woman called Amessis or Amensis. This woman was later identified by historians as Hatshepsut. At this point in history, records of the reign of Hatshepsut end, since the first major foreign campaign of Thutmose III was dated to his 22nd year, which also would have been Hatshepsut's 22nd year as pharaoh.

Dating the beginning of her reign is more difficult. Her father's reign began in either 1526 or 1506 BCE according to the high and low estimates of her reign. The length of the reigns of Thutmose I and Thutmose II, however, cannot be determined with certainty. With short reigns, Hatshepsut would have ascended the throne 14 years after the coronation of Thutmose I, her father. Longer reigns would put her ascension 25 years after Thutmose I's coronation.

The earliest attestation of Hatshepsut as pharaoh occurs in the tomb of Ramose and Hatnofer, where a collection of grave goods contained a single pottery jar or amphora from the tomb's chamber - which was stamped with the date "Year 7". Another jar from the same tomb – which was discovered in situ by a 1935–36 Metropolitan Museum of Art expedition on a hillside near Thebes – was stamped with the seal of the "God's Wife Hatshepsut" while two jars bore the seal of "The Good Goddess Maatkare." The dating of the amphorae, "sealed into the [tomb's] burial chamber by the debris from Senenmut's own tomb", is undisputed, which means that Hatshepsut was acknowledged as pharaoh, and not queen, of Egypt by Year 7 of her reign.

Building projects

Hatshepsut was one of the most prolific builders in Ancient Egypt, commissioning hundreds of construction projects throughout both Upper Egypt and Lower Egypt. Many of these building projects were temples to build her religious base and legitimacy beyond her position as God's Wife of Amun. At these temples, she performed religious rituals that had hitherto been reserved for kings, corroborating the evidence that Hatshepsut assumed traditionally male roles as pharaoh. She employed the great architect Ineni, who also had worked for her father, her husband, and for the royal steward Senenmut. The extant artifacts of the statuary provide archaeological evidence of Hatshepsut's portrayals of herself as a male pharaoh, with physically masculine traits and traditionally male Ancient Egyptian garb, such as a false beard and ram's horns. These images are seen as symbolic, and not evidence of cross-dressing or androgyny.

Following the tradition of most pharaohs, Hatshepsut had monuments constructed at the Temple of Karnak. She also restored the original Precinct of Mut, the great ancient goddess of Egypt, at Karnak that had been ravaged by the foreign rulers during the Hyksos occupation. It later was ravaged by other pharaohs, who took one part after another to use in their own projects. The precinct awaits restoration. She had twin obelisks erected at the entrance to the temple which at the time of building were the tallest in the world. Only one remains upright, which is the second-tallest ancient obelisk still standing, the other having toppled and broken in two. The official in charge of those obelisks was the high steward Amenhotep. Another project, Karnak's Red Chapel, or Chapelle Rouge, was built as a barque shrine.

Later, she ordered the construction of two more obelisks to celebrate her 16th year as pharaoh; one of the obelisks broke during construction, and a third was therefore constructed to replace it. The broken obelisk was left at its quarrying site in Aswan, where it remains. Known as the Unfinished Obelisk, it provides evidence of how obelisks were quaried.

Hatshepsut built the Temple of Pakhet at Beni Hasan in the Minya Governorate south of Al Minya. The name, Pakhet, was a synthesis that occurred by combining Bast and Sekhmet, who were similar lioness war goddesses, in an area that bordered the north and south division of their cults. The cavernous underground temple, cut into the rock cliffs on the eastern side of the Nile, was admired and called the Speos Artemidos by the Greeks during their occupation of Egypt, known as the Ptolemaic Dynasty. They saw the goddess as akin to their hunter goddess, Artemis. The temple is thought to have been built alongside much more ancient ones that have not survived. This temple has an architrave with a long dedicatory text bearing Hatshepsut's famous denunciation of the Hyksos that James P. Allen has translated. This temple was altered later, and some of its insides were altered by Seti I of the Nineteenth Dynasty in an attempt to have his name replace that of Hatshepsut.

Following the tradition of many pharaohs, the masterpiece of Hatshepsut's building projects was a mortuary temple. She built hers in a complex at Deir el-Bahri. The identity of the architect behind the project remains unclear. It is possible that Senenmut, the Overseer of Works, or Hapuseneb, the High Priest, were responsible. It is also likely that Hatshepsut provided input to the project. Located opposite the city of Luxor, it is considered to be a masterpiece of ancient architecture. The complex's focal point was the Djeser-Djeseru or "the Holy of Holies".

Queen Hatshepsut at the Deir el-Bahri temple in Luxor

Mother remembers Queen Hatshepsut

Standing in front of a portrait of Queen Hatshepsut, the Mother told us the following story when she came to the library of the Sri Aurobindo Ashram in Pondicherry, India, to open an exhibition on "Ancient Egypt" in August 1954.

When she was a girl of about eight or ten, she and her brother were taken one day by her teacher to the famous Louvre Museum in Paris.

On the ground floor are galleries of the Egyptian antiquities. As they were slowly passing through the collections, the Mother was suddenly attracted by a beautiful toilet-case inlaid with gold and lapis lazuli, which was exposed in one of the museum cases. An attendant noticed her great interest and explained to her that the toilet-case had once belonged to the Egyptian Queen Hatshepsut.

He also showed her a fine portrait of the Queen as a young girl and smilingly remarked that she had a striking resemblance to that ancient Queen. The toilet-case, and particularly the comb, appeared to be strangely familiar to the Mother. About 3,500 years ago, Queen Hatshepsut ascended the throne of Egypt at a time when the word 'Queen' did not exist. She was the first woman to rule over Egypt. In the hieroglyphic inscriptions she was designated as 'the King' and called 'Female Horus'. The word 'Majesty' was put in feminine form for the first time. On solemn occasions she had to wear a pointed beard, the exclusive sign of royalty of the Pharaohs.

Beautiful and talented, she became famous for her extensive building activities, an entirely new style of architecture was developed during her reign. The imposing rock temple of Hatshepsut, now known as Deir-el-Bahri, was built by her. The energetic Queen sent to the ends of the known world expeditions for fruit trees and flowers to be planted on the terraces of that temple of God. The gigantic shaft of her Karnak obelisk stands even today as a monument to her greatness.

Medhananda, Mother India, June 1958

Queen Hatshepsut, Neues Museum, Berlin

The Mother's reincarnations in Egypt

"Do you not know, Asclepius, that Egypt is an image of heaven? Or, so to speak more exactly, that in Egypt all the operations of powers which rule and work in heaven have been transferred down to the earth below?" (Hermeticum)[1]

The Mother has said that she had had 'at least' three incarnations in Egypt.

Her contact with Egypt started when she was very young, at the Guimet Museum in Paris. When she was asked many years later by a child why accidents often happen to people who break into the tombs in Egypt, she answered abruptly: 'They deserve it!' Then she added: 'Let me explain. In the physical form is contained "the spirit of the form," and this spirit of the form remains for some time, even when outwardly the person is declared dead. As long as the spirit of the form persists, the body does not decompose. In ancient Egypt they had this knowledge. They knew that if they prepared the body in a certain manner, the spirit of the form would not leave it and the body would not disintegrate. In some cases they have succeeded wonderfully well. And if one disturbs the repose of beings who have remained like that for thousands of years, I understand that they are not very pleased, especially when their repose is disturbed out of unhealthy curiosity, justified in the name of science.

'In the Guimet Museum, in Paris, there are two mummies. Of the one nothing much is left, but in the other the spirit of the form

---

1   Robert Bauval and Graham Hancock, *Keeper of Genesis*
    Quoted from the *Corpus Hermeticum*

has remained very conscious, to such an extent that one can have a contact by means of the consciousness. It goes without saying that it cannot be very pleasant when a bunch of idiots come and stare at you with popping eyes understanding nothing and saying all the time: "Look, he is like this! Look, he is like that!" ... Given the fact that it was never ordinary people who were mummified; these were beings who had realized a considerable inner power or who were members of the royal family, persons more or less initiated. There is a mummy which has been the cause of a large number of catastrophes. She was a princess, daughter of a pharaoh, and secretly at the head of a college of initiation at Thebes.'[2] The warning inscribed over some tombs, 'Death shall come on swift wings to him that toucheth the tomb of the Pharaoh,'[3] seems not to have been a vain threat.

The Mother said that ancient Egypt was extremely occult. Now this begins to be understood more widely. Robert Bauval and Graham Hancock, for instance, write in their Keeper of Genesis: 'From available primary sources, the overall picture that emerges is that the "Followers of Horus" may not have been "kings" in the usual sense of the word but rather immensely powerful and enlightened individuals – high initiates who were carefully selected by an elite academy that established itself at the sacred site of Heliopolis-Giza thousands of years before history began.'[4]

Standing in front of a portrait of Queen Hatshepsut, the Mother told the following story when she came to the Ashram's University Centre Library to open an exhibition on ancient Egypt in August 1954. When she was a girl of about eight or ten, she and her

---

2   The Mother, *Questions and Answers 1950-51,* CWM 4:196-97
3   Graham Philips, *Act of God*
4   Robert Bauval and Graham Hancock, *Keeper of Genesis*

Amenhotep III and Tiye, Akhenaten's parents
at the Egypt Museum, Cairo

brother were taken one day by her teacher [more probably their nanny, Miss Gatliffe] to the famous Museum of the Louvre in Paris. On the ground floor are galleries of Egyptian antiquities. As they were slowly passing through the collections, the Mother was suddenly attracted by a beautiful toilet case inlaid with gold and lapis lazuli, which was exposed in one of the museum cases. An attendant noticed her great interest and explained to her that the toilet case had once belonged to the Egyptian Queen Hatshepsut. He also showed her a fine portrait of the Queen as a young girl and smilingly remarked that she had a striking resemblance to that ancient Queen. The toilet case and particularly the comb appeared to be strangely familiar to the Mother.'[5] It is reasonable to suggest that the Mother would not have told this anecdote if there was no profound reason for it. Besides, we have already mentioned that the Mother experienced an affinity with Queen Hatshepsut in 1914, during her visit to a museum in Cairo, en route to Pondicherry.

It is most often thought that Hatshepsut (ca. 1504-ca. 1483)[6] has been the only Egyptian queen to reign as a king. Yet, this happened four or five times, for example in the case of Netokris (ca. 2160), Sobeknofru (ca. 2160), Ankhet-kheperu-re (ca. 1347) and Tauseret (ca. 1186). In all these cases, however, the rule of the female pharaoh was rather short, while Hatshepsut, whose name means 'the Foremost of Women,' ruled for about twenty-two years and her reign marked one of the highlights of Egyptian civilization.

---

5   *Glimpses of the Mother's Life I*

6   Unfortunately, nothing in Egyptology can ever be taken for granted,' writes Joyce Tyldesley. This is particularly true for the dates of the reign of kings and queens, each authority coming up with a different proposal based on his or her own excellent reasons. The sequence of events within a reign, however, is well-known, as the Egyptian scribes dated these events with reference to the first year of the reign

'Among the kings of the XVIIIth dynasty', writes Jean Yoyotte, 'Hatshepsut is, together with Akhenaten, the one who evokes the most admiration, amazement and questions.'[7]

'Queen or, as she would prefer to be remembered, King Hatshepsut ruled during 18th Dynasty Egypt for over twenty years,' writes Joyce Tyldesley. 'Her story is that of a remarkable woman. Born the eldest daughter of King Thutmosis I, married to her half-brother Thutmosis II, and guardian of her young stepson-nephew Thutmosis III, Hatshepsut somehow managed to defy tradition and establish herself on the divine throne of the pharaohs. From this time onwards Hatshepsut became the female embodiment of a male role, uniquely depicted both as a conventional woman and as a man, dressed in male clothing, carrying male accessories and even sporting the traditional pharaoh's false beard. Her reign, a carefully balanced period of internal peace, foreign exploration and monumental building, was in all respects – except one obvious one – a conventional New Kingdom regime; Egypt prospered under her rule.'[8]

Hatshepsut married her half-brother Thutmosis II when she was about fourteen or fifteen years of age, thus becoming 'the Great Princess, great in favour and grace, Mistress of All Lands, Royal Daughter and Royal Sister, Great Royal Wife, Mistress of the Two Lands [i.e. Upper and Lower Egypt].' Her royal husband died young, and was succeeded by her nephew, Thutmosis III, who was still a child. Hatshepsut became his regent and therefore the highest authority in the realm. But then Hatshepsut sprang a surprise: in the seventh year of the boy's reign she proclaimed herself Pharaoh, or rather had herself proclaimed thus by an oracle of Amon, the

---

7   Jean Yoyotte, in *Historia*
8   Joyce Tyldesley, *Hatshepsut - The Female Pharaoh*

chief god and presiding deity of the huge temples in Luxor and Karnak, the temple in which she was crowned. She became 'the Female Horus, the king of Upper and Lower Egypt, Maatkare, the son of Re, Hatshepsut-Khnemet-Amun! May she live forever!'

The reason for this unconventional and bold step is unknown. It may be supposed, however, that she took the crown of the Two Lands because for some reason or other the succession of the dynasty was in peril, her husband having died prematurely and the new king still being a child. It should be realized that, for the Egyptians, their Pharaoh was literally a god on earth, who upheld Maat, that is the Dharma of the land, who made the sun rise and the river Nile come into spate, and who sustained the life of all beings. Joyce Tyldesley makes a telling comparison between Hatshepsut and Queen Elizabeth I of England, 'a woman who inherited her throne against all odds at a time of dynastic difficulty when the royal family was suffering from a shortage of sons, and who deliberately stressed her relationship with her vigorous and effective father in order to lessen the effect of her own femininity and make her own reign more acceptable to her people.'[9]

The proof of Hatshepsut's insight and strength in daring the practically impossible is the success of her reign as King Maatkare. (Re being the Sun, Ka the divine force in all, and Maat the same as Maya or Dharma, the name could be translated as 'Maat is the vital Force of Re,' or, in terms more familiar to us, as 'Shakti of the Sun' – the Sun being the symbol of the divine Unity-Consciousness, the Supramental.) Thanks to her, Egypt, which had been partially ruined by the invasion of the Hyksos only half a century before, became prosperous again. Peace reigned within the country and with all its neighbours. 'I have given you the pacification within the

---

9   Joyce Tyldesley, *Hatshepsut - The Female Pharaoh*

provinces and every town is quiet,' she proclaimed. Great building works were undertaken, and so were expeditions to foreign lands. Hatshepsut became 'the most influential woman ever known' and her reign 'the most fruitful period ever in Egypt.' She 'stands out as one of the great monarchs of Egypt.'

In the temple of Karnak Hatshepsut had two gigantic obelisks erected. The process of their being hewn out of the rock, in the south of the country, of their transportation and erection is shown on the walls of Deir el-Bahri. After something like three and a half millenniums, one of these obelisks is still standing. The top of it was covered with shining electrum, a mixture of gold and silver. Thus were the rays of Re, the Sun, reflected over the country during its daily course from dawn to dusk and its yearly course through the seasons. It must have been a splendid sight.

And then there was the temple at Deir el-Bahri, Hatshepsut's mortuary temple, called Djeser-Djeseru: 'Holy of Holies' – 'beyond doubt one of the most beautiful buildings in the world,' and generally recognized as such. 'It is built at the base of the rugged Theban cliffs [on the west bank of the Nile], and commands the plain in magnificent fashion: its white colonnades rising, terrace above terrace, until it is backed by the golden living rock. The ivory-white walls of courts, side chambers and colonnades have polished surfaces which give an alabaster-like effect. They are carved with a fine art, figures and hieroglyphs being filled in with rich yellow colour, the glow of which against the whites gives an effect of warmth and beauty quite indescribable.[10] (J.R. Buttles).

Although the architect of Djeser-Djeseru seems to have been Hapuseneb, the supervisor and creator of the masterwork was Senenmut, the famous assistant of Hatshepsut, acting on her direct

---

10 Joyce Tyldesley, *Hatshepsut - The Female Pharaoh*

Temple of Queen Hatshepsut, Deir el-Bahari, Luxor

inspiration. 'I was the greatest of the great in the whole land,' say the hieroglyphs in Senenmut's tomb. 'I was guardian of the secrets of the King [that is Hatshepsut] in all his places: a privy councillor on the Sovereign's right hand, secure in favour and given audience alone. I was one upon whose utterances his Lord relied, with whose advice the Mistress of the Two Lands was satisfied, and the heart of the Divine Consort was completely filled.'[11] It is interesting to note how Hatshepsut had picked out a whole team of able collaborators to run the kingdom. Senenmut, her assistant, architect Hapuseneb, Chancellor Neshi, leader of the expedition to Punt, the Treasurer Thuthmosis, Useramen the vizier, Amenhotep the chief steward, Inebni, Viceroy of Kush, and others. Again one is reminded of Elizabeth I of England and her court. The Mother would probably have said that this group of outstanding collaborators belonged to 'the family'.

The reign of the extraordinary Queen Hatshepsut was a period of peace, prosperity and stabilization. It was the basis upon which Thutmosis III, when he finally became Pharaoh in his own right, expanded the kingdom. He became known as 'the Egyptian Napoleon' and waged no less than seventeen victorious campaigns. Hatshepsut's work in reviving the prosperity of the land would render Tiye and Akhenaten's astounding reformation possible. Who has hacked away her effigies and the cartouches containing her royal name? Nobody can tell with any certainty. For the Egyptians the power of the written or chiseled word or hieroglyph was very real, as was the power of the statues and buildings. An erasure of a name or the mutilation of a statue was a direct attack on the Ka, and thus on the survival of the person represented by the hieroglyphs or the statue. Strange to say, the memory of King Hatshepsut was

---

11 Joyce Tyldesley, *Hatshepsut - The Female Pharaoh*

obliterated for many centuries from Egyptian history and only rediscovered in the nineteenth century.

Georges Van Vrekhem,
The Mother, The Story of Her Life

Queen Tiye

'About two years ago,' the Mother said in May 1956, 'I had a vision in connection with Z's son. She had brought him to me – he was not quite one year old – so I had just seen him in the room where I receive people. He gave me the impression of someone very well known to me, but I didn't know who or what. Then, in the afternoon of the same day [during her midday rest], I had a vision. It was a vision of ancient Egypt, and I was somebody there: I was the High Priestess, or whomever. I didn't know whom, for [during the experience] one doesn't tell oneself "I am so-and-so." The identification is complete, there is no objectivation, so I don't know.

'I was in an admirable building, immense! so high! – but quite bare. There was nothing, except a place with magnificent paintings, which I recognized as the paintings of ancient Egypt. I was coming out of my apartments and entering a kind of large hall. There was a sort of gutter all along the walls, for collecting the water. And then I saw the child, half naked, playing in it. I was quite shocked. I said: "What is this! This is disgusting!" (The feelings, ideas and all that were translated into French in my consciousness.) Then the tutor came – I had him called. I gave him a scolding. I heard the sounds. I don't know what I said, I don't remember the sounds any more. I heard the sounds I was pronouncing, I knew their meaning, but the translation was in French and the sounds I didn't remember. I spoke to [the tutor], I told him: "How can you let the child play in there?" He answered – and I woke up with his reply – saying . . . I did not hear the first words, but in my thought it was [translated as]: "Amenhotep likes it." "Amenhotep" I heard and I remembered. Then I knew the little one had been Amenhotep.

Queen Tiye wife of Amenhotep III and Mother of Akhenaten

'So I know that I spoke. I spoke in that language, but I don't remember it now. I remembered "Amenhotep" because I have kept that in my active consciousness: "Amenhotep". But the rest, the other sounds did not remain. I have no memory for sounds. And I know I was his mother. Then I knew who I was, for I know that Amenhotep was the son of so-and-so. Besides, I looked it up in history.'[12]

As the Mother has confirmed afterwards, that child, her son, was Amenhotep 1V (1376-47),[13] the future Akhenaten, which means that she was Queen Tiye (1397-1360). Tiye, though her father occupied a high position in the realm, was not of royal blood and possibly of Nubian descent. She had been chosen in 1389 as his principal consort by Amenhotep III, the Magnificent. 'The name of her father is Yuya, the name of her mother is Tuya. She is the spouse of a powerful king whose southern border reaches to Karoy and his northern to Naharin,'[14] is the way the Pharaoh had the high status of his wife proclaimed throughout the Two Lands. Tiye became the mother of Amenhotep IV (1376-47), who afterwards, in one of the most spectacular religious reformations in history, would call himself Akhenaten and found the city of Akhet-Aten.

'Tiye had a very powerful influence on her husband Amenhotep III. Her strong personality dominated the mentally weaker king completely. As a queen, she decided about the broad outlines within the structure of his policy and played an important role in the Egyptian religious life. Amenhotep III already felt the power of

---

12 The Mother, *Questions and Answers 1956,* CWM 8:155-56
13 For the dates concerning this section on Queen Tiye and Amenhotep IV, Akhenaten, we follow De Mummie van Nofretete by Arnold Berbers and Hendrik Beumer (1988). The name Amenhotep is the same as Amenophis
14 Arnold Berbers and Hendrik Beumer, *De Mummie van Nofretete*

the sun god Aton, and it is in no way improbable that Tiye took the initiative to stimulate his dormant sympathy for this god.'[15] The sun god Aton, never represented in human form but as the sun disk, was central to the theology of Heliopolis, perhaps the most ancient in Egypt, although he played only a minor role in the official religion. That Amenhotep and Tiye were profoundly dedicated to Aton is shown by the fact that he was revered in their palace at Malgatta, west of Thebes, and that the boat in which Tiye moved on the huge artificial lake her husband had dug for her was called 'Aton radiates'.

Most historians agree that Tiye had an equally strong influence on her son Amenhotep IV. As Berbers and Beumer write: 'Through his mother Tiye, in this supported by his father Amenhotep III, he must have been initiated in the philosophies around Aton and indoctrinated with the idea that for the religious salvation of Egypt a god like Aton was the only outcome.'[16] This influence must have been very strong indeed, for after his father had died, Amenhotep IV changed his name into Akhenaten, translated variously as 'he who is faithful to Aten,' 'one useful to Aten,' 'he who serves Aten' and 'reflection of Aten.' And not only did he change his name, he founded a totally new city, Akhet-Aten, 'Horizon of Aten,' on the right bank of the Nile, halfway between Thebes and Memphis. The name of the city may be understood as the projection of the Sun World into the material world of the earth.

This splendid city, entirely dedicated to the new creed, was built in an incredibly short time and must have been a costly enterprise. Akhenaten lived there with his wife, the famous Nefertiti ('the Beautiful has come') and their six daughters. There he worshipped

15 Ibid. p. 63
16 Arnold Berbers and Hendrik Beumer, *De Mummie van Nofretete*

Amenhotep III, Queen Tiye's husband and Father of Akhenaten
Luxor Museum

the sun disk, represented by the ankh, the sign of life, and little hands blessing all existence. And there he received also his mother Tiye, who had remained in her palace at Malgatta, but who would breathe her last, in 1347, in that fantastic city which had probably arisen under her impulse.

Akhenaten's revolutionary undertaking – he has been called 'the heretic king' and 'the most controversial of all kings of Egypt' – went completely against the established and extremely powerful religion of the time, and is considered the first attempt at monotheism. The faceless Aton was declared the only God and the worship of all other gods, of the whole Egyptian pantheon, was abolished. The significance of this act can only be understood if one realizes that the priestly caste was second in power to the Pharaoh – who was a living god, the incarnated Horus on earth – and often vied with him for supremacy. The temple of Amon in Thebes had become one of the richest in Egypt, and the power of the Amon priests was still on the increase. 'By the middle of the New Kingdom, the religious foundations controlled an estimated one-third of the cultivated land and employed approximately twenty per cent of the population . . . Within a very short time the Amon temple at Karnak was second only to the throne itself as a centre of economic and political influence in Egypt.'[17] Their wrath at Akhenaten's reformist acts must have been unforgiving.

And unforgiving it was. There seem to have been signs of the decline of Akhenaten even towards the end of Akhenaten's brief life. (Life was generally brief in those times.) After his death in 1347, and while Nefertiti was still living in her palace at Akhet-Aten, the brand-new city gradually emptied of its population. When Nefertiti died in 1344, her son Tutankhaton could or would no

---

17 Joyce Tyldesley, *Hatshepsut - The Female Pharaoh*

Queen Tiye, wearing the crown with cattle horns and a solar disk.
The hawks feathers transform the queen into a goddess.

longer resist the conservative powers; he changed his name into Tutankhamen and, together with his wife, went back to Thebes. In 1333 General Horemheb became Pharaoh. This was the end of the XVIIIth Dynasty – and of the City of the Sun, which he razed to the ground with the fury only religious fanaticism can inspire. It disappeared under the desert sands and for many centuries there was nothing to be seen but a hill at a place called Tell el-Amarna.

Modern historians have little or no understanding of what happened at the time of Tiye, Akhenaten and Nefertiti. The reason is that they project their world view and even their religious prejudices on times and events that were utterly different from the ones in which they live. As the Mother said, the life, culture and religion of ancient Egypt were determined by an exceptional presence of the occult. What is occult is by definition unknown. It is worthwhile pointing out that many of the prominent Greeks – Solon, Pythagoras, Herodotus, Plato – found the sources of their knowledge in Egypt (which means that European culture has its roots deeper than Greece, in the Kingdom of the Two Lands).[18] All of these Greeks were instructed by representatives of the Egyptian priesthood, but as the latter were bound by their vows, the knowledge they shared was but a part of what they actually knew. Only recently has there been an effort among Western scholars to approach ancient Egypt with less arrogance and with more patience and openness when seeking the still hidden sources of that civilization.

---

18 It is also worth pointing out that Moses was instructed by the Egyptian priesthood, as is written in the Acts of the Apostles (7:22), and may have been an initiate. Thus another source of Western civilization, the Semitic, goes back to the Land of the Nile.

The impulse, the force Tiye, Akhenaten and Nefertiti (who also was totally dedicated to the Aton) were drawing from, must have been very powerful indeed to allow for a revolution such as the one brought about. Looking back on it from the viewpoint of Sri Aurobindo and the Mother, one may assume the following. Tiye was a 'Vibhuti' of the Universal Mother, a fact which endowed her with the awareness of her eternal soul within, and thus of the Divine. She had probably become an initiate of the mysteries of Heliopolis, keeper of the secrets of the Sun. Here it is worth mentioning that Sri Aurobindo said that the Sun is the symbol of the Supramental, which is the Divine upholding all creation. (This upholding and blessing is graphically represented in Akhenaten's iconography of the Sun disk.) Having become a high occult initiate, Tiye may have had the vision or inspiration – or a series of visions or inspirations – of the supramental Truth. The word 'supramental Truth' is nothing but a verbal abstraction for a divine Reality which surpasses everything an ordinary human being can feel, imagine and experience. It is the One Reality present in all that exists and of which the gods are the cosmic powers.

Tiye may have had some kind of realization of the Supramental and transmitted it to her husband, son and daughter-in-law. Nothing short of such a realization could have been powerful enough to enable these few individuals, however elevated their position, to undertake the steps we have read about against the stubborn, conservative, centuries-old established powers and customs. Graham Philips writes: 'Indeed, [the Aton] is unlike any Egyptian god: an all powerful, heavenly father who demands that his children live in 'truth.' Precisely what this reference to truth implies is hard to say. One can only assume that Akhenaten's followers were encouraged to behave candidly and live an honest life. The word Maat, 'Truth', appears again and again at Amarna,

Queen Hatshepsut, at the Deir el-Bahri temple in Luxor

and the phrase 'living in truth' seems almost to have been a motto of the new religion.'[19] It is also a key concept in the Yoga of Sri Aurobindo and the Mother.

Tanmaya, a French teacher for many years at the Sri Aurobindo Ashram school recalls, in reply to a question (concerning Akhenaten) he had put to the Mother:

"Mother let it clearly be understood that she had been Queen Tiye, the mother of Akhenaten ... she specified that Akhenaten's revolution was intended to reveal to the people of that time the Unity of the Divine and his Manifestation".

This attempt, the Mother added, was premature,

for the human mind was not yet ready for it.

It had, however, to be undertaken in order to assure

the continuity of its existence in the mental plane.

The Mother, The Story of Her Life, Georges Van Vrekhem

---

19 Graham Philips, *Act of God*

The Beginning of History for Israel

K. D. Sethna (Amal Kiran), born as a Parsi in Bombay on 25th November 1904 – 29th June 2011, came first time to Pondicherry in 1927 and stayed at the Ashram for several years. He permanently settled in Pondicherry in 1954 and has lived there ever since. He was a distinguished writer, his works covering poetry, literary criticism, history, Christianity, philosophy and of course Sri Aurobindo and the Mother. He published more than 50 books. He was also the editor of the monthly journal Mother India.

Revolutionizing Ancient History: The Case of Israel and Christianity

Becoming a poet, a political commentator, a literary critic while editing a monthly journal of culture without stirring out of an ashram in South India may not be a matter provoking comment let alone arousing wonder. But to revolutionize the very chronology of the ancient world based on minute examination of the latest archaeological findings and texts from within such confines - that, too, in the pre-internet era - could not but astonish. It becomes all the more amazing when the subject is not just the prehistory of one's own country but so distant a subject as the beginnings of history for Israel and Christianity. ...

Taking his point of departure from the 1968 lectures Professor Chaim Rabin of Hebrew University delivered in India placing the Exodus of the Israelites from Egypt in the mid-13th century BCE, Sethna, in *The Beginning of History for Israel* challenges this

as well as archaeologist W.F. Albright's dating of the Exodus to
c, 1294 BCE and his identification of the Pharaoh responsible for
this as Ramses II. While painstakingly taking Albright apart over
227 pages, Sethna also takes on - and demolishes - a completely
different type of antagonist who is himself denounced by orthodox
historians as "the other" because of his revolutionary reading of
Egyptian history: Immanuel Velikovsky, notorious author of *Worlds
in Collision* and *Ages in Chaos. ...*

... Sethna fixes on the "Pharaoh's daughter" who brought
up Moses as the famous Hatshepsut, daughter of Amenophis I
(1546-1525 BCE), with Moses being born in 1521 BCE and she
dying in 1482 BCE to be succeeded by Tuthmosis III. ...

... Sethna expands on the unique role of Hatshepsut - inevitably,
when we recall that she is supposed to have been one of the Mother's
avatars - to show that Moses' monotheism had its roots in the new
religion of Amon that she established, merging all the temples into
a single organization. He points out how Moses' dialogue with God
in the burning bush episode echoes the colloquy between Amon,
speaking from his shrine about God's land and living among the
trees there, and Hatshepsut. ...

Dr. Pradip Bhattacharya

The Date of the Exodus

Now we have to ascertain what Pharaoh or Pharaohs are needed for the whole table (of approximate dates). Here the important factor is the famous Queen-Pharaoh Hatshepsut, daughter of Tuthmois I and half-sister of Tuthmosis II. Murrays reports: "At the end of his reign Thothmes I associated his daughter Hatshepsut with himself as co-regent. In her records she claims to have reigned as king, but the official lists ignore her altogether, and place Tuthmosis II as the immediate successor of Tuthmosis I." Whatever the situation after Tuthmosis I, there is no question about her kingship at the death of her half-brother. Because of Tuthmosis III's minority she was appointed regent. Manchip White says: "During the course of the regency her appetite for power became so inordinate that she boldly mounted the throne and declared herself Pharaoh." Hayes calculates: "A text at Karnac describes Hatshepsut's assumption of the kingship in Year 2 of Tuthmosis III. Her disappearance from history some time between the 20th and 22nd years agrees with Manetho's slightly garbled statement that after the third king of the dynasty 'his sister Amessis' ruled for twenty-one years and nine months." So Hatshepsut's reign would be in 1503-1482 BCE. Before she declared herself Pharaoh, she is most likely to have filled the role of "the daughter of Pharaoh" to whom the Bible ascribes the discovery of baby Moses "in an ark of bulrushes. in the flags by the river's brink" *(Exodus 2:3)*.

With Moses born in 1521 BCE and Hatshepsut's father Tuthmosis I wearing the crown in 1525 BCE, how old would we expect her to be at the time of the discovery? The answer would hang on when the marriage of which she was the offspring took place. We read in Manchip White about her father: "Tuthmosis was the son of Amenophis by a concubine, but he rapidly reinforced his claim to the throne by marrying his half-sister Ahmosis, daughter of his father by his legitimate queen." Murray, with a slight variation, says substantially the same thing: "his mother was a lady of the royal family though not the heiress. His right to the kingship was obtained, as was usual at this period, by marriage with the heiress." F. Llewellyn Griffith steers a middle course towards the identical. fact: "Tuthmosis I...was perhaps of another family, but obtained his title to the throne through his wife Ahmosi" - and Llewellyn Griffith adds the information that Hatshepsut was Tuthmosis I's daughter by Ahmosi. The scholar writing in the *Encyclopedia Britannica* of 1977, after mentioning that "the title of God's Wife was... bestowed upon the principal heiress in childhood, and the pharaoh customarily married the most legitimate heiress to validate his right to the throne", goes on to present the proper situation regarding Tuthmosis I: "Lacking a surviving heir, Amenhotep I was succeeded by one of his generals, Thutmose I (ruled 1525-c.1512 BCE), who had married the royal heiress and God's Wife Ahmose." The cumulative suggestion appears clearly to be that Tuthmosis I made sure of his right in advance of his predecessor's death so that no question may arise afterwards. How much in advance cannot be said with certainty, but we may hazard a guess in the light of the general practice. Manchip White says: "The future Pharaoh was married in childhood to the most suitable of his small sisters, half-sisters or cousins. When he was a man he was permitted to take as many additional wives and mistresses as he desired, but it was essential that his immediate heir should possess the strongest possible strain of royal blood." Obviously, even if there was no child-marriage within the same family, Tuthmosis I was joined to the right partner sufficiently early in life to get round the inconvenience of his inferior birth and to consolidate his claim to succession. We gather from Manchip White that ancient Egypt was "a country where a woman bore her first child at the age of twelve and seldom produced less than six or seven all told". Somewhere in the midst of the reign of Amenophis I (1546-1525 BCE), the future king must have got married to the heiress in time for her child-bearing age. So his daughter Hatshepsut must have been born fairly before his own enthronement in 1525 BCE and she was old enough when Moses, a baby of 3 months, was discovered and the "pharaoh's daughter" got the child nursed by a Hebrew woman who happened to be its own mother and when, after "the child grew up", it was brought to "pharaoh's daughter and he became her son" (*Exodus 2:7-10*). Actually she is required to be no more than 12 years old, the age at which she could be ready either to bear a son or to adopt one. And surely, all circumstances considered, Hatshepsut was not of less age than the minimum. ...

It seems no accident that the Dynasty, to which the Bible's estimate of the date of the Exodus from Solomon's 4th year leads us, has a notable "daughter of pharaoh" who is fit in every way to do what the Bible describes. Hatshepsut proves the greatest aid to our chronology.

We shall return to this celebrated woman and further elucidate her possible relationship with Moses and his message. At the moment we must consider her father, grandfather and brother in relation to the Israelites. Her father Tuthmosis I, whom Murray calls "one of the great warrior kings of Egypt" as well as the inaugurator of "that wonderful era of temple-building which lasted until the XXth dynasty", becomes the originator of the decree that all male children should be drowned in the Nile. And, as Moses' elder brother Aaron, born 3 years earlier, was not under any threat, the decree must have been passed after 1524 BCE (the year of Aaron's birth) and before or in the year - 1521 when Hatshepsut found

Tuthmosis I, father of Queen Hatshepsut

Moses. If it was in 1521, the few years earlier of Tuthmosis I's reign which started in 1525 must have been concerned with scrutinising the outcome of the command to the Hebrew midwives. Whether he or his father gave the command cannot be decided. Perhaps in the decree which touched on Moses he may have merely continued the anti-Israelite policy of his father.

In any case the years between 1525 and 1521 are too short a period for all the measures adopted previous to it and for the study of their consequences. The measures must go into the reign of Amenophis I (1546-1525 BCE) - a long enough time to set them in motion and examine their effects. What we have to ask is: "Was Amenophis I likely to go in for those measures?"

The reason the Bible gives for the Oppression is the excessive multiplication of the children of Israel. The Pharaoh says: "Come on, let us deal wisely with them; lest they multiply, and it come to pass that, when there falleth out any war, they join also unto our enemies, and fight against us." (*Exodus*, 1:10.) The situation Amenophis I faced was just the one which would prompt such a statement. Murray 7 recounts how "Aahmes" (his father) fought those foreigners, the Hyksos, who had already been pushed northward by his brother "Kames" (better known as Kamosis) and how on Kames's death he "drove the enemy to the confines of Egypt, and finally chased them out of the country". Then, after telling of his other campaigns and noting his strong physique from his mummy, he" writes: "Aahmes was succeeded by his son Amenhotep I. The Hyksos were still a danger to Egypt for they were strong enough to attempt to regain their lost conquest, and they were near the northern frontier of Egypt. Amenhotep was forced to fight in more than one campaign against them...'." In expectation of an attack by the watching and none-too-far Hyksos, he might with special reason suspect the loyalty of the

Hebrews who were located on one side of the very frontier on whose other side were the expelled enemy. And the fear of their turning "quislings" would be distinctly augmented by the facts narrated by Albright' in relation to the Hyksos: "That there was a long Semitic occupation of the north-eastern Delta before the New Empire [established by 'Aahmes' of the 18th Dynasty] is certain from the Canaanite place-names found there in the New Empire, which include Succoth, Baal-Zephon, Migdol, Zilu (Sillo) and probably Goshen itself. That there were a good many Semites among Hyksos officials is certain, and it is also clear that most of the Hyksos chiefs bore Semitic names, among which is Ya-gob-har (literally, 'May the Mountain-god Protect'), formed with the same element as 'Jacob'." The Hebrews, themselves Semites, could undoubtedly appear to the son of the founder of the 18th Dynasty as a great danger in case of renewed war with the Hyksos. We may also remember that the Hyksos are known, from a tradition handed down by Manetho, as "Shepherd Kings" and that the Hebrews when they first came into Egypt were told by Joseph who was then the vizier there: "I will go up, and see Pharaoh, and may say unto him, My brethren, and my father's house, which were in the land of Canaan, are come unto me: And the men are shepherds... And it shall come to pass, when Pharaoh shall call you, and shall say, What is your occupation? that ye shall say, 'Thy servants' trade hath been about cattle from our youth even until now, both we, and also our fathers: that we may dwell in the land of Goshen: for every shepherd is an abomination unto the Egyptians'" (*Genesis* 46:31-34).

While Amenophis I suits the part of the initiator Oppressive Pharaoh with the appropriate circumstances and both Tuthmosis I and Hatshepsut are rightly where they are, what of her brother, Tuthmosis II who followed her father on the throne? He is really a shadowy figure. Murray characterises him: "He was a great contrast to his predecessor, for he seems to have been a weakling, somewhat effeminate with his artificially curled brown hair... This was no great warrior leading his men to battle and being found always in the thickest of the fight, but a rather timorous young man who could make a brave show when he could sit on his throne in all the panoply of royalty, and put his foot on the necks of bound and helpless prisoners." With Hatshepsut appointed by Tuthmosis I as co-regent in the last part of his reign, it would seem that Tuthmosis II was only a fellow-co-regent, but officially he was a successor and is reckoned as such in the lists. We can also see that he inherited something of the mind of the two Pharaohs before him: the one who had commanded the mid-wives to kill the male offspring of the Hebrew women and the other who had charged "all his people, saying, Every son that is born ye shall cast into the .." Murray 75 reports about Tuthmosis II: "When the news was brought that 'the miserable Kush have begun to rebel, his Majesty raged like a panther of the South. Said his Majesty, 'I swear as Re loves me, as Amon favours me, I shall not leave one of their males alive'."

Here the question crops up: "In spite of Tuthmosis I and Tuthmosis II how could Hatshepsut bring up Moses so that, as the Bible says, 'he became her son'?" The answer must be: "As Moses was brought up in the royal household and, as his very name which is of Egyptian derivation suggests, he was exceptionally regarded as a non-Hebrew and the persisting persecution did not touch him. Then there is not only the innate power of Hatshepsut's character but also her influence over her father to the extent that she was co-regent with him for a while until he died and that the co-regency gave her the right to stand on her own legs during the official kingship of Tuthmosis II. Besides, she was, as

Tuthmosis II, the younger brother of Queen Hatshepsut
Egyptian Museum, Turin, Italy

Manchip White lets us know, not only Tuthmosis II's half-sister but also his wife. Llewellyn Griffith referring to Tuthmosis I, says: 'A son, Tuthmosis II, succeeded as the husband of his half-sister Hatshepsut. Associated with her, Moses lived protected all through the two reigns."

Even when Tuthmosis III was officially proclaimed Pharaoh in 1504 BCE, she continued to be a presence to be reckoned with. She was both his aunt and his mother-in-law. Llewellyn Griffith relates that Tuthmosis III was the son of Tuthmosis II by a concubine Esi, and Manchip White, while dubbing Tuthmosis III "the illegitimate son of a concubine", discloses that Hatshepsut got her nephew married "to her own daughter by Tuthmosis II". The daughter bore her mother's name, so that we find Amenophis I calling himself the son not only of Tuthmosis III but also of Hatshepsut. What contributed most to the senior Hatshepsut's dominant position and made her more independent than ever when Tuthmosis III was put on the throne was that he was a minor and she could act the full Pharaoh now. Even though he came of age a few years later, she persisted in that role until her death in 1482 BCE. In the Bible, as in the Egyptian official records, she is not recognised as a ruler, but we can see that it is only when "the daughter of Pharaoh" disappears from the scene and someone else is at the top that Moses, grown up, "went out unto his brethren, and looked on their burdens" and committed the offence which occasioned the Biblical passage: "Now when pharaoh heard this thing, he sought to slay Moses" (Exodus 2:15). The Pharaoh involved we may identify with Tuthmosis III who came into his own on Hatshepsut's demise. So we have four Pharaohs of the Oppression - Amenophis I, Tuthmosis I, Tuthmosis II and Tuthmosis III - and not merely two as we may superficially gather from the Bible's frequently condensed, "jumpy" and telescoping narrative.

At this point it will be pertinent to spotlight a small yet not insignificant area of agreement between the Bible's story of Moses and our identification of Tuthmosis III as the fourth Pharaoh of the Oppression. If Hatshepsut died in 1482 BCE, the time when Moses was out of her protection can be calculated by deducting 1482 from his birth-date 1521: we get the age of 39 years. Subsequent to her death he would get into contact with his fellows and have in the course of it the experience the Bible records: "...he espied an Egyptian smiting an Hebrew. And he looked this way and that way, and when he saw that there was no man, he slew the Egyptian and hid him in the sand" (*Exodus* 2:11-12). As soon as his violent act was discovered his life was in danger from the enraged Pharaoh and "Moses fled from the face of Pharaoh, and dwelt in the land of Midian" (*Exodus* 2:15).

The tradition about the time of Moses' life when he had to flee to Midian is the background to Gaston Maspero's statement: "Moses had already attained forty years of age when he one day encountered an Egyptian smiting a Hebrew and slew him...." Albright' compares to "the life of Moses" the 120-year-long life of "Argenthonius, king of Tartessus in the sixth century BCE," which was divided into "three periods of a generation each" - namely, 40 years, as several ancient peoples including the Israelites reckoned a generation. The Acts of the Apostles, in the New Testament, openly voices the old tradition about Moses: "And when he was full forty years old, it came into his heart to visit his brethren, the children of Israel" (7:23). That Moses, by our calculation, should have become 40 very soon after and not any time before Hatshepsut's death and got exposed to a Pharaoh's threat to his life is one more indication of our having calculated rightly.

Quite a contrast meets us if we make Ramses II the Pharaoh of the Exodus and still more if he is the Pharaoh of both the

Tuthmosis III, successor of Queen Hatshepsut

Oppression and the Exodus. With the Exodus set in c. 1294 BCE and with Moses 80 in this year, he could not have been born in the reign of Ramses II, who started ruling in 1304 BCE and allegedly oppressing the Jews forthwith. Or, if he was born, he would be 10 years old at the Exodus, already a father of children by then and a man-slaughterer while a toddling infant! Even supposing with the school of Mayani as well as Albright that Ramses II was the Pharaoh of the Exodus and Seti I the Pharaoh of the Oppression, Moses in order to be 80 in 1294 would have to be born in 1373 - before Seti I's reign (1319-1305 BCE) - and would pass clean beyond the current scheme.

Here let us throw a general glance at the consonance of the historical Hatshepsut's life and mind with the attitude of Moses' liberal feminine patron in the Bible and with the religious mission of this leader of the Israelites.

Murray sums up Hatshepsut's personality and achievement: "She was a woman of great force of character; and if her portraits speak true, she was endowed with beauty and charm as well. Her reign is characterised by the great expansion of trade, and by her passionate devotion to her religion which showed itself in the creation of one of the finest temples that even Egypt can boast of, and by the decoration of other temples as well." If she was the saviour of Moses, the Jews might justly look back to her with the utmost reverence and attach special significance to the sculpture - illustrated inscriptions on the walls of her magnificent temple at Deir el Bahri, inscriptions that "recount among other things the story of her divine birth". And the Jews might also remember the special turn the religious spirit of Egypt takes under her. The 18th Dynasty of which she was an early member was one of empire-builders. Already in her day the Egyptian mind was stretched far and wide beyond the borders of the country. As she herself claimed:

"My southern boundary is as far as Punt...; my eastern boundary is as far as the marshes of Asia, and the Asiatics are in my grasp; my western boundary is as far as the mountain of Mani [the sunset]... my fame is among the Sand-dwellers [the Bedouin] altogether. The myrrh of Punt has been brought to me... All the goodly sweet woods of God's-Land.' Along with the imperial extension from the Third Cataract of the Nile to the Euphrates there went the sense of divinity at universal work. Particularly was that sense active in relation to the mysterious region called Punt, which, before Hatshepsut, had received Egyptian expeditions but with nothing more than the most meagre allusions to it.

It is Hatshepsut who brought Punt into prominence, making almost a cult of it, so to speak. She refers in one of her inscriptions to the fact that the god Amon inspired her to "establish for him Punt in his house". Breasted tells the story: "...one day as the queen stood before the shrine of the god, a command was heard from the great throne, an oracle of the god himself, that the ways to Punt should be searched out, that the highways to the myrrh-terraces should be penetrated. For, so says the god, 'it is a glorious region of God's-Land, it is indeed my place of delight; I have made it for myself in order to divert my heart.' The queen adds, 'it was done according to all that the majesty of this god commanded.' "When the great venture was over, she reminded her ministers of Amon's oracle commanding her "to plant the trees of God's-Land beside his temple in his garden", and she proudly continued: "It was done.... I have made for him a Punt in his garden, just as he commanded. It is large enough for him to walk abroad in it."

The colloquy between Amon and Hatshepsut, the deity speaking out of his shrine and from his garden about God's-Land and residing ultimately among the trees from that glorious region - all this sends out distant connections with the story of Moses and the burning bush: "...God called unto him out of the midst of the bush, and said, Moses, Moses. And he said, Here am I. And he said, Draw not hither: put off thy shoes from thy feet, for the place whereon thou standest is holy ground... And the Lord said, I have surely seen the affliction of my people which are in Egypt.... And I am come down...to bring them out of that land unto a good land and a large land, unto a land flowing with milk and honey (*Exodus* 3:4-5, 7, 8).

Again, Hatshepsut's Amon, already identified with the Sun-god Re, was a presence that had gained supremacy in the Egyptian pantheon. Nor was this confined to theological theory. "Economically and administratively," Breasted reports, "Amon actually received the first place among the gods." For the first time in the history of the country, the priesthoods of all the temples of the land were merged into "one great sacerdotal organisation", at the head of which stood the High Priest of Amon. Tuthmosis III is often credited with having effected the merger and raised to a peak the High Priest's status. Knowing that Tuthmosis, during his boyhood, was placed in Amon's temple at Karnak as a priest with the rank of prophet and that the Amon-priesthood was his staunch supporter, we cannot dissociate him from the new organization. But the first pontifex maximus of this organization was Hapuseneb who was Hatshepsut's grand vizier. Thus it was during the joint rule of Hatshepsut and Tuthmosis that the Amonite papacy was established. After the Queen's death, not only did Tuthmosis mutilate her works and erase her name, but "a statue of the vizier Hapuseneb was treated in the same way." So the economic and administrative supremacy of Amon-Re must have been inspired by Hatshepsut and the widely presiding singleness of his divinity must have drawn its initial strength from her. Here was the first stirring of a universalist and monotheistic theology. If Moses was Hatshepsut's protégé, it is most apt that we should find him to be the first explicit and unquestionable monotheist among the Hebrews, with Jehovah saying to him: "Thou shalt have no other gods before me" (Exodus 20:3). His mind could have been quickened by the new movement to receive the revelation in the land of Midian where he had fled a few years after the Queen's demise. ...

The role of a Pharaoh of the Oppression appears well played in several respects by Tuthmosis III, who hated the peace-loving yet independent-minded Hatshepsut so much that after her death "everywhere he had her name erased and in the terraced temple on all the walls both her figure and her name have been hacked out." Tuthmosis III, "this little, squat, plump-faced man whose mummified features can still be studied in the Cairo Museum' - "the fore-head....abnormally low, the eyes deeply sunk, the jaw heavy, the lips thick, and the cheek-bones extremely prominent" - "a fellah of the old stock...vulgar in character and expression, but not lacking in firmness and vigour' or deficient in resourcefulness," marked as his mummy is "with the intelligent face recognisable from his statues, the whole height of the body no more than about 5 feet 3 inches? yet no more negligible than Napoleon's shortness of stature - this rather unattractive-looking but sharp-witted storehouse of stupendous energy, relentless leader of seventeen successful campaigns, the mightiest conqueror in Egyptian history, whose name was a terror in Palestine and Syria and Lebanon and even as far as the Euphrates.

However, we must not ignore another side of his personality. Murray paints a picture which seems the very opposite of his role as oppressor of the Israelites: "Tuthmosis was not only a great general, but a statesman as well with high ideals. His treatment of conquered countries was always humane; even the chiefs who fought against him were not executed, they were merely deposed."

"The sons of the princes and their brothers were brought to be placed as hostages in Egypt. If any one of the chiefs died, his Majesty would make his son to stand in his stead." He established the Pax Aegyptica over the whole of his empire; no longer were there plundering expeditions by one little kinglet against another little kinglet; Syria and Palestine were forced to keep the peace, and under his benign rule they reached a degree of prosperity which they have seldom, if ever, enjoyed."

All this could be quite true and yet he might oppress the Israelites because of the suspicions we have mentioned. And once his mistrust was aroused, the very forcefulness of his character would make him fierce. And he could be fierce with the Jews in spite of the virtues that Breasted in his turn attributes to him. Breasted attends to what Rekhmire, the vizier who stood closest to Tuthmosis, says of him: "Lo, his majesty was one who knew what happened; there was nothing of which he was ignorant; he was Thoth [the god of knowledge] in everything; there was no matter which he did not carry out." Breasted also relates that, while he was proud to leave behind a record of his unparallelled achievement, Tuthmosis protests more than once his deep respect for the truth in so doing. Then Breasted quotes him: "I have not uttered exaggeration in order to boast of that which I did, saying, 'I have done something', although my majesty had not done it. I have not done anything...against which contradictions might be uttered. I have this for my father, Amon...because he knoweth heaven and he knoweth earth, he seeth the whole earth hourly."

Breasted's reference to the ethico-religious bent of Tuthmosis III is very suggestive in connection with our making this Pharaoh a contemporary of the grown-up Moses. Moses, we have said, is the first outstanding Hebrew monotheist. And we have pointed out the monotheistic turn the Egyptian religious spirit took under

Tuthmosis III, successor of Queen Hatshepsut
Egyptian Museum, Cairo

Hatshepsut. Tuthmosis III, we may remind ourselves, was co-regent with her for about 20 years and, though he wreaked vengeance upon her memory and on that of Hapuzeneb, the first High Priest of the Amonite papacy which she had set up in collaboration with Tuthmosis, the merger of all priesthoods continued during his sole sovereignty. Egyptian religion assumed even a stronger monotheistic colour during his reign. The difference became still more marked between the old Amon-Re and the new one about whom this Pharaoh uses the closing words of our last quotation: "He seeth the whole earth hourly." Breasted pictures the Egyptian empire as a religious unity achieved by means of the sword of Tuthmosis III. "Tuthmosis III," says Breasted, "was the first character of universal aspects, the first world-hero... The idea of universal power, of a world-empire, was visibly and tangibly bodied forth in his career. There is a touch of universalism now discernible in the theology of the Empire which is directly due to such impression as he and his successors made... It was universalism expressed in terms of imperial power which first caught the imagination of the thinking men of the Empire, and disclosed to them the universal sweep of the Sun-god's dominion as a physical fact. Monotheism is but imperialism in religion."

Often the Aten-cult which developed under Akhenaten, the great-grandson of Tuthmosis III, is described as the dawn of monotheism in Egypt. Actually the dawn is in the reign of Hatshepsut, and the full morning in that of Tuthmosis III: what Akhenaten brought about, while revolting against Amon-Re, was the intensification - under a heterodoxical form - of the monotheistic spirit kindled three generations earlier. Albright recognizes this very well when he casts about for a background to Hebrew monotheism in non-Hebrew literature. "The most striking passages," he tells us, "naturally come from Egypt, where our sources are much more extensive. Since the

Aten heresy was a special development, we shall restrict ourselves here to the great Egypt Amun hymn of the 15th century..." Then he quotes from the hymn. We shall reproduce a few passages in his translation:

"Thou far-traveller, thou prince of Upper Egypt, Lord of the land of the Matoi (Eastern Desert of Nubia) and ruler of Punt (East Africa).

"Thou greatest of heaven, thou eldest of the earth, lord of what exists.

"Legitimate lord, father of the gods, who created man and made the animals.

"Thou art the only one, who created what there is; the unique one, who created what exists - thou from whose eyes came men and from whose mouths sprang the gods.

" 'Praise to thee!' (says) every wild animal. 'Hail to thee!' (says) every foreign land, *as high as heaven and as wide as Earth is and as deep as the sea is."* ...

Amal Kiran (K. D. Sethna)
The Beginning of History for Israel

Pharaoh Akhenaten
Colossal statue from Karnak

Table of Approximate Dates*
The Beginning of History for Israel

Israelite History	Egyptian History

Israelite History

Abraham, aged 75, leaves Haran
in north-western Mesopotamia
for Canaan.

2085 BC

Abraham goes to Egypt.

2081/2080 BC

Joseph becomes grand vizier in Egypt
at the age of 30.

1878 BC

Advent of the Israelites under Joseph's
father Jacob into Egypt.

1870 BC

Death of Jacob.   **1854 BC**

Period of the Hyksos.

1720–1570 BC

Beginning of the Oppression
of the Israelites.

Birth of Moses, who as a baby is put on
the Nile's bank in a basket but is picked
up on the order of "the daughter of Pharao"
by her maids.

1520 BC

Egyptian History

Egypt was divided between
the Heracleopolitan 10th Dynasty under
Acthoes III and the Theban 11th Dynasty
under Inyotef II.

Sesostris III of the 12th Dynasty
is on the throne of Egypt.

1878–1843 BC

Ahmosis, 1st ruler of the 18th Dynasty,
founder of the New Kingdom.

1570–1546 BC

Amenophis I, 2nd ruler
of the 18th Dynasty,
first "Pharaoh of the Oppression".

1546–1525 BC

Tuthmosis I, second
"Pharaoh of the Oppression"
and father of Hatshepsut
who is then an Egyptian princess.

1525–1512 BC

Tuthmosis II, brother of Hatshepsut
and third "Pharaoh of the Oppression".

1512–1504 BC

Hatshepsut, ruler from the 2nd year
of the kingship of Tuthmosis III
who as a minor of 6 comes to the throne
and whose regent she is.
1503–1482 BC

Moses, 39, kills a cruel Egyptian overseer
of the Israelite slave-labour gang
and flees to Midian.
1482 BC

Tuthmosis III, at last ruler on his own, is
the fourth "Pharaoh of the Oppression".
1482–1450 BC

Moses, 80, returns to Egypt
at God's command
and leads the Exodus of the Israelites.
1441 BC

Amenophis II,
the "Pharaoh of the Exodus".
1450–1424 BC

The Israelites, after wandering in the
wilderness for 40 years, enter Palestine
under Joshua and take Jericho soon after
the death of Moses at the age of 120 in
sight of the Promised Land.
1401 BC

Amenophis III, whose reign practically
covers the first 10 years
of the period of the EI Amarna Letters
(1389-1358 B.C.).
1415–1379 BC

The reign of Amenophis IV (Akhenaten)
covering the next 17 years of the Letters.
1379–1362 BC

Smenkhare. **1362–1361 BC**

The reign of Tutankhamen,
covering most of the last
4 years of the Letters.
1361–1351 BC

The Fall of Debir. **1350 BC**

AY **1351–1348 BC**

The Fall of Bethel. **1325 BC**

Horemheb **1348–1320 BC**

Ramses I, founder of 19th Dynasty.
1320–1319 BC

Seti I **1319–1304 BC**

The Fall of Hazor	**1275 BC**	Ramses II	**1304-1238 BC**
The Fall of Lachish	**1230 BC**	Merneptah	**1238-1225 BC**
		Amenmesses	**1225-1220 BC**
		Ramses III	**1198-1165 BC**

Saul **1011-1003 BC**

David **1003-964 BC**

Solomon who was visited by the Queen
of Sheba with precious gifts.
964-925 BC

Solomon's 4th regnal year which is said
in I *Kings* 6:1 to be 480 years later than
the Exodus to mark the starting-point of
his construction of the Temple.
961 BC

Solomon's son Rehoboam in whose
5th year the Egyptian King Shishak
conquers Jerusalem and carries away the
treasures of the Temple and the palace.
921 BC

Sheshonk I, founder of the 22nd
Libyan Dynasty who is equated to
the Biblical Shishak.
935–914 BC

* The Egyptian dates follow W.C Hayes in Chronolgy - *Egypt;
Western Asia; Aegean Bronze Age*, pp.17-19.

Queen Cleopatra VII, *Thea Philopator*

The Mother, unlike Sri Aurobindo, has spoken about her past incarnations, some of which she has described in some detail. According to her, her very first birth in a human form was in the earthly paradise about which she has spoken in detail in works:

On Thoughts and Aphorisms. She has spoken of having 'at least' three births in Egypt; among them she has spoken at length about two and the source of the information regarding the third birth is Amal Kiran (K.D. Sethna).

The incarnations were Queen Hatchepsut (1504–1483 BCE), Queen Tiye (1397–60 BCE)
and Queen Cleopatra (January 69–12 August 30 BCE), the Hellenistic ruler of Egypt who shared power first with her father Ptolemy XII and later with her brothers/husbands Ptolemy XIII and Ptolemy XIV.

✷

According to K.D. Sethna, the Mother was also born as Queen Cleopatra, but we don't know whether the Mother herself has said anything about this particular incarnation of hers.

✷

Sri Aurobindo was once asked by one of his young disciples, Nagin Doshi, what he and the Mother had been doing in their former births. "Carrying on the evolution" was the answer that he received from his Guru. When asked to elaborate, Sri Aurobindo wrote back: "That would mean writing the whole of human history.

I can only say that as there are special descents to carry on the evolution to a farther stage, so also something of the Divine is always there to help through each stage itself in one direction or another."

*

Both Sri Aurobindo and the Mother took birth to foster the progress of evolution of mankind, and in each birth they played a very significant role. Each birth was unique in its own way: sometimes they came as rulers, sometimes as warriors and sometimes as artists or philosophers. As artists, their artistic creations are still admired; as philosophers, their works are still read even after the passing of several centuries. As rulers and warriors, their contribution to the society is still remembered. But what remain unknown are the former incarnations of Sri Aurobindo and the Mother. Sri Aurobindo has always been very silent about his past births, but compared to him the Mother was more expressive and she spoke about her former births only in passing. As a matter of fact she, along with Nolini Kanta Gupta, has been the primary source of information about hers and Sri Aurobindo's previous incarnations. In the following pages we shall discuss about their former births based on the information they themselves have provided.

The Light of the Supreme, Journals,
"The former Incarnations of Sri Aurobindo and the Mother",
April 20th 2009, by Anurag Banerjee

Cleopatra VII Thea Philopator (Koinē Greek: lit. Cleopatra "father-loving goddess"; 70/69 BC – 10 August 30 BC) was Queen of the Ptolemaic Kingdom of Egypt from 51 to 30 BC, and its last active ruler. A member of the Ptolemaic dynasty, she was a descendant of its founder Ptolemy I Soter, a Macedonian Greek general and companion of Alexander the Great.

After the death of Cleopatra, Egypt became a province of the Roman Empire, marking the end of the last Hellenistic period state in the Mediterranean and of the age that had lasted since the reign of Alexander (336–323 BC).

Although her first language was Koine Greek, she was the only Ptolemaic ruler to learn and use the Egyptian language.

In 58 BC, Cleopatra presumably accompanied her father, Ptolemy XII Auletes, during his exile to Rome after a revolt in Egypt (a Roman client state) allowed his rival daughter Berenice IV to claim his throne. Berenice was killed in 55 BC when Ptolemy returned to Egypt with Roman military assistance. When he died in 51 BC, the joint reign of Cleopatra and her brother Ptolemy XIII began, but a falling-out between them led to open civil war. After losing the 48 BC Battle of Pharsalus in Greece against his rival Julius Caesar (a Roman dictator and consul) in Caesar's civil war, the Roman statesman Pompey fled to Egypt.

Pompey had been a political ally of Ptolemy XII, but Ptolemy XIII, at the urging of his court eunuchs, had Pompey ambushed and killed before Caesar arrived and occupied Alexandria. Caesar then attempted to reconcile the rival Ptolemaic siblings, but Ptolemy's chief adviser, Potheinos, viewed Caesar's terms as favoring Cleopatra, so his forces besieged her and Caesar at the palace.

Shortly after the siege was lifted by reinforcements, Ptolemy XIII died in the Battle of the Nile; Cleopatra's half-sister Arsinoe

IV was eventually exiled to Ephesus for her role in carrying out the siege.

Caesar declared Cleopatra and her brother Ptolemy XIV joint rulers but maintained a private affair with Cleopatra that produced a son, Caesarion. Cleopatra traveled to Rome as a client queen in 46 and 44 BC, where she stayed at Caesar's villa. After the assassination of Caesar and (on her orders) Ptolemy XIV in 44 BC, she named Caesarion co-ruler as Ptolemy XV.

In the Liberators' civil war of 43–42 BC, Cleopatra sided with the Roman Second Triumvirate formed by Caesar's grandnephew and heir Octavian, Mark Antony, and Marcus Aemilius Lepidus.

After their meeting at Tarsos in 41 BC, the queen had an affair with Antony. He carried out the execution of Arsinoe at her request, and became increasingly reliant on Cleopatra for both funding and military aid during his invasions of the Parthian Empire and the Kingdom of Armenia. The Donations of Alexandria declared their children Alexander Helios, Cleopatra Selene II, and Ptolemy Philadelphus rulers over various erstwhile territories under Antony's triumviral authority.

This event, their marriage, and Antony's divorce of Octavian's sister Octavia Minor led to the final war of the Roman Republic. Octavian engaged in a war of propaganda, forced Antony's allies in the Roman Senate to flee Rome in 32 BC, and declared war on Cleopatra.

After defeating Antony and Cleopatra's naval fleet at the 31 BC Battle of Actium, Octavian's forces invaded Egypt in 30 BC and defeated Antony, leading to Antony's suicide.

Queen Cleopatra, a Roman sculpture wearing a royal diadem,
mid-1st century BC (around the time of her visits to Rome in 46-44 BC)
discovered in an Italian villa
along the Via Appia and now located in the Altes Museum, Berlin.

When Cleopatra learned that Octavian planned to bring her to his Roman triumphal procession, she killed herself by poisoning, contrary to the popular belief that she was bitten by an viper (Asp).

Cleopatra's legacy survives in ancient and modern works of art. Roman historiography and Latin poetry produced a generally critical view of the queen that pervaded later Medieval and Renaissance literature.

In the visual arts, her ancient depictions include Roman busts, paintings, and sculptures, cameo carvings and glass, Ptolemaic and Roman coinage, and reliefs. In Renaissance and Baroque art, she was the subject of many works including operas, paintings, poetry, sculptures, and theatrical dramas.

She has become a pop culture icon of Egyptomania since the Victorian era, and in modern times, Cleopatra has appeared in the applied and fine arts, burlesque satire, Hollywood films, and brand images for commercial products.

The remains of the Mansion of Aten
Coordinates 27⁰ 38' 43.58" N, 30⁰ 53' 44.30" E

Auroville Yesterday?

"Here is the place which belongs to no prince, to no god.

No one owns it.

Here is the place for all of us...

The earth will find joy in it.

Here the hearts will be happy."

Does this sound familiar?

You may have heard about the beautiful queen of Egypt, Nefertiti. She was born in 1388 BCE and was married to the Pharaoh Amenophis IV, later known as Akhenaten. Akhenaten was a daring reformist. He opted for a monotheist cult, in a time of polytheism. He only worshipped the LIGHT, pure and free.

In 1369 BCE, this "modern" couple founded the new city of *Amarna*, which means Horizon. It became the capital of Egypt. It was situated midway between Memphis (Cairo) and Thebes (Luxor), on the eastern bank of the Nile.

At this place, the cliffs of the high desert shift away from the river and form a wide hemicircle of fertile soil, some 12 kms long and a bit less than 5 kms wide. Big steles (flat pillars) were put around the area, bearing the story of its foundation.

At the centre of the city, Akhenaten and Nefertiti built a temple to the Light. Inside, there was no picture of any god and no image of traditional worshipping.

In this new city, Akhenaten wanted everybody to be equal: Egyptians and foreigners (many of whom were attracted there), kings and common people, men and women. Artists and craftsmen received support and encouragement to express their skills fully. Money was not the sovereign ruler. Soldiers did other jobs than war.

Akhenaten and Nefertiti, followed by one of their daughters, present offerings to their god Aten, who is represented by a solar disk the rays of which terminate in hands, Stela of the Eighteenth Dynasty, 1580 to 1350 BCE. Cairo.

It went on for 22 years, amidst growing discontent of the traditional ruling classes, the army chiefs and the polytheist high priests.

When the general-dictator Horemheb seized power in 1347 BCE, he revived the old capital Thebes and sent thousands of troops to Amarna with one goal: total obliteration. Graves were mutilated, buildings demolished, the names of Akhenaten and Nefertiti were frenziedly chipped from the walls. The city was virtually razed to the ground. A layer of cement was spread over the ruins, as if to make sure that no contamination from this cursed place could ever occur.

Only the upper Castle remained untouched. The Queen Nefertiti, who helplessly witnessed everything, found refuge there with her scribe Bubastos.

This story perhaps gives Auroville a new dimension; was it the same spirit that passed unscathed from Egypt through the centuries to be materialized again here in India?

Gilbert Lachaux

Auroville Today, April 1989
Reference "Nefertiti et Ie reve d'Akhenaten", by André Chedid

Pharaoh Horemheb, general and dictator who has sent his troops to Akhet-Aten for a total demolition.

Akhenaten's life: A Brilliant Flash of Light

Akhenaten was an ancient Egyptian pharaoh reigning c.1351–1334 BCE, the tenth ruler of the Eighteenth Dynasty. Before the fifth year of his reign, he was known as Amenhotep IV.

As a pharaoh, Akhenaten is noted for abandoning Egypt's traditional polytheism and introducing Atenism, or worship centred around Aten. The views of Egyptologists differ as to whether the religious policy was absolutely monotheistic, or whether it was monolatry, syncretistic, or henotheistic. This culture shift away from traditional religion was reversed after his death. Akhenaten's monuments were dismantled and hidden, his statues were destroyed, and his name excluded from lists of rulers compiled by later pharaohs. Traditional religious practice was gradually restored, notably under his close successor Tutankhamun, who changed his name from Tutankhaten early in his reign. When some dozen years later, rulers without clear rights of succession from the Eighteenth Dynasty founded a new dynasty, they discredited Akhenaten and his immediate successors and referred to Akhenaten as "the enemy" or "that criminal" in archival records.

Akhenaten was all but lost to history until the late 19th century discovery of Amarna, or Akhet-Aten, the new capital city he built for the worship of Aten. Furthermore, in 1907, a mummy that could be Akhenaten's was unearthed from the tomb KV55 in the Valley of the Kings by Edward R. Ayrton. Genetic testing has determined that the man buried in KV55 was Tutankhamun's father, but its identification as Akhenaten has since been questioned.

Akhenaten's rediscovery and Flinders Petrie's early excavations at Amarna sparked great public interest in the pharaoh and his queen Nefertiti. He has been described as "enigmatic", "mysterious",

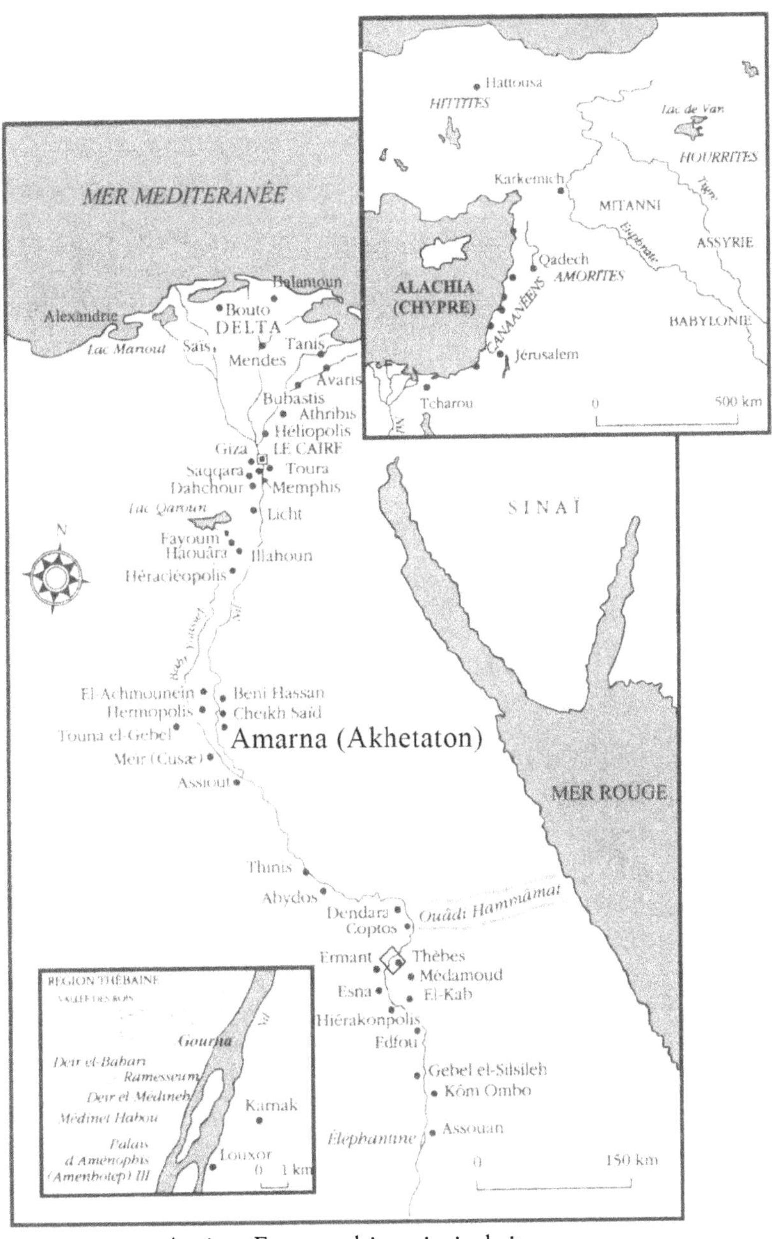

Ancient Egypt and its principal sites

Akhenaten praying to Aten together with his wife Nefertiti
and their daughters.

"revolutionary", "the greatest idealist of the world", and "the first individual in history", but also as a "heretic", "fanatic", "possibly insane", and "mad". Public and scholarly fascination with Akhenaten comes from his connection with Tutankhamun, the unique style and high quality of the pictorial arts he patronized, and the religion he attempted to establish, foreshadowing monotheism.

Family

The future Akhenaten was born Amenhotep, a younger son of pharaoh Amenhotep III and his principal wife Tiye. Akhenaten had an elder brother, crown prince Thutmose, who was recognized as Amenhotep III's heir. Akhenaten also had four or five sisters: Sitamun, Henuttaneb, Iset, Nebetah, and possibly Beketaten, Thutmose's early death, perhaps around Amenhotep III's thirtieth regnal year, meant that Akhenaten was next in line for Egypt's throne.

Akhenaten was married to Nefertiti, his Great Royal Wife. The exact timing of their marriage is unknown, but inscriptions from the pharaoh's building projects suggest that they married either shortly before or after Akhenaten took the throne. For example, Egyptologist Dimitri Laboury suggests that the marriage took place in Akhenaten's fourth regnal year. A secondary wife of Akhenaten named Kiya is also known from inscriptions. Some Egyptologists theorize that she gained her importance as the mother of Tutankhamun. William Murnane proposes that Kiya is the colloquial name of the Mitanni princess Tadukhipa, daughter of the Mitanni king Tushratta who had married Amenhotep III before becoming the wife of Akhenaten. Akhenaten's other attested consorts are the daughter of the Enišasi ruler Šatiya and another daughter of the Babylonian king Burna-Buriash II.

Akhenaten could have had seven or eight children based on inscriptions. Egyptologists are fairly certain about his six daughters, who are well attested in contemporary depictions. Among his six daughters, Meritaten was born in regnal year one or five; Meketaten in year four or six; Ankhesenpaaten, later queen of Tutankhamun, before year five or eight; Neferneferuaten Tasherit in year eight or nine; Neferneferure in year nine or ten; and Setepenre in year ten or eleven. Tutankhamun, born Tutankhaten, was most likely Akhenaten's son, with Nefertiti or another wife. There is less certainty around Akhenaten's relationship with Smenkhkare, Akhenaten's coregent or successor and husband to his daughter Meritaten; he could have been Akhenaten's eldest son with an unknown wife or Akhenaten's younger brother.

Early life as prince Amenhotep

Egyptologists know very little about Akhenaten's life as prince Amenhotep. Donald B. Redford dates his birth before his father Amenhotep III's 25th regnal year, c. 1363–1361 BCE, based on the birth of Akhenaten's first daughter, who was likely born fairly early in his own reign. The only mention of his name, as "the King's Son Amenhotep," was found on a wine docket at Amenhotep III's Malkata palace, where some historians suggested Akhenaten was born. Others contend that he was born at Memphis, where growing up he was influenced by the worship of the sun god Ra practiced at nearby Heliopolis.

Akhenaten took Egypt's throne as Amenhotep IV, most likely in 1353. It is unknown how old Amenhotep IV was when he did

Queen Nefertiti, an artifact from the master sculptor
Thutmose's workshop in Akhet-Aten.

this; estimates range from 10 to 23. He was most likely crowned in Thebes, or less likely at Memphis or Armant.

The beginning of Amenhotep IV's reign followed established pharaonic traditions. He did not immediately start redirecting worship toward the Aten and distancing himself from other gods. Egyptologist Donald B. Redford believes this implied that Amenhotep IV's eventual religious policies were not conceived of before his reign, and he did not follow a pre-established plan or programme. Redford points to three pieces of evidence to support this. First, surviving inscriptions show Amenhotep IV worshipping several different gods, including Atum, Osiris, Anubis, Nekhbet, Hathor, and the Eye of Ra, and texts from this era refer to "the gods" and "every god and every goddess."

The High Priest of Amun was also still active in the fourth year of Amenhotep IV's reign. Second, even though he later moved his capital from Thebes to Akhet-Aten, his initial royal titulary honoured Thebes – his nomen was "Amenhotep, god-ruler of Thebes" – and recognizing its importance, he called the city "Southern Heliopolis, the first great (seat) of Re (or) the Disc." Third, Amenhotep IV did not yet destroy temples to the other gods and he even continued his father's construction projects at Karnak's Precinct of Amun-Re. He decorated the walls of the precinct's Third Pylon with images of himself worshipping Ra-Horakhty, portrayed in the god's traditional form of a falcon-headed man. Artistic depictions continued unchanged early in Amenhotep IV's reign. Tombs built or completed in the first few years after he took the throne, such as those of Kheruef, Ramose and Parennefer, show the pharaoh in the traditional artistic style. In Ramose's tomb, Amenhotep IV appears on the west wall, seated on a throne, with Ramose appearing before the pharaoh. On the other side of the doorway, Amenhotep IV and Nefertiti are shown in the window of appearances, with the Aten depicted as the sun disc. In Parennefer's tomb, Amenhotep IV and Nefertiti are seated on a throne with the sun disc depicted over the pharaoh and his queen.

While continuing the worship of other gods, Amenhotep IV's initial building programme sought to build new places of worship to the Aten. He ordered the construction of temples or shrines to the Aten in several cities across the country, such as Bubastis, Tell el-Borg, Heliopolis, Memphis, Nekhen, Kawa, and Kerma. He also ordered the construction of a large temple complex dedicated to the Aten at Karnak in Thebes, northeast of the parts of the Karnak complex dedicated to Amun. The Aten temple complex, collectively known as the Per Aten ("House of the Aten"), consisted of several temples whose names survive: the Gempaaten ("The Aten is found in the estate of the Aten"), the Hwt Benben ("House or Temple of the Benben"), the Rud-Menu ("Enduring of monuments for Aten forever"), the Teni-Menu ("Exalted are the monuments of the Aten forever"), and the Sekhen Aten ("booth of Aten").

Around regnal year two or three, Amenhotep IV organized a Sed festival. Sed festivals were ritual rejuvenations of an aging pharaoh, which usually took place for the first time around the thirtieth year of a pharaoh's reign and every three or so years thereafter. Egyptologists only speculate as to why Amenhotep IV organized a Sed festival when he was likely still in his early twenties. Some historians see it as evidence for Amenhotep III and Amenhotep IV's co-regency, and believed that Amenhotep IV's Sed festival coincided with one of his father's celebrations. Others speculate that Amenhotep IV chose to hold his festival three years after his father's death, aiming to proclaim his rule a continuation of his father's reign. Yet others believe that the festival was held to honour the Aten on whose behalf the pharaoh ruled Egypt, or, as Amenhotep III was considered to have become one with the Aten

Prince Akhenaten, an artifact from the master sculptor
Thutmose's workshop in Akhet-Aten, Neues Museum, Berlin.

following his death, the Sed festival honoured both the pharaoh and the god at the same time. It is also possible that the purpose of the ceremony was to figuratively fill Amenhotep IV with strength before his great enterprise: the introduction of the Aten cult and the founding of the new capital Akhet-Aten. Regardless of the celebration's aim, Egyptologists believe that during the festivities Amenhotep IV only made offerings to the Aten rather than the many gods and goddesses, as was customary.

Name change from Amenhotep IV to Akhenaten

Amenhotep IV changed his royal titulary to show his devotion to the Aten. No longer would he be known as Amenhotep IV and be associated with the god Amun, but rather he would completely shift his focus to the Aten. Egyptologists debate the exact meaning of Akhenaten, his new personal name. The word "akh" could have different translations, such as "satisfied," "effective spirit," or "serviceable to," and thus Akhenaten's name could be translated to mean "Aten is satisfied".

Founding Akhet-Aten (Tell el-Amarna)

Around the same time he changed his royal titulary. On the thirteenth day of the growing season's fourth month, Akhenaten decreed that a new capital city be built: Akhet-Aten "Horizon of the Aten", better known today as Amarna. The event Egyptologists know the most about during Akhenaten's life are connected with founding Akhet-Aten, as several so-called boundary stelae were found around the city to mark its boundary. The pharaoh chose a site about halfway between Thebes, the capital at the time, and Memphis, on the east bank of the Nile, where a wadi and a natural dip in the surrounding cliffs form a silhouette similar to the "horizon" hieroglyph. Additionally, the site had previously been uninhabited. According to inscriptions on one boundary stela, the site was appropriate for Aten's city for "not being the property of a god, nor being the property of a goddess, nor being the property of a ruler, nor being the property of a female ruler, nor being the property of any people able to lay claim to it."

Historians do not know for certain why Akhenaten established a new capital and left Thebes, the old capital. The boundary stelae detailing Akhet-Aten's founding is damaged where it likely explained the pharaoh's motives for the move. Surviving parts claim what happened to Akhenaten was "worse than those that I heard" previously in his reign and worse than those "heard by any kings who assumed the White Crown," and alludes to "offensive" speech against the Aten. Egyptologists believe that Akhenaten could be referring to conflict with the priesthood and followers of Amun, the patron god of Thebes. The great temples of Amun, such as Karnak, were all located in Thebes and the priests there achieved significant power earlier in the Eighteenth Dynasty, especially under Hatshepsut and Thutmose III, thanks to pharaohs offering large amounts of Egypt's growing wealth to the cult of Amun; historians, such as Donald B. Redford, therefore posited that by moving to a new capital, Akhenaten may have been trying to break with Amun's priests and the god. Akhet-Aten was a planned city with the Great Temple of the Aten, Small Aten Temple, royal residences, records office, and government buildings in the city centre. Some of these buildings, such as the Aten temples, were ordered to be built by Akhenaten on the boundary stela decreeing the city's founding.

Pharaoh Akhenaten, wearing the Double Crown of Egypt
Colossal statue of Akhenaten

Akhenaten died after seventeen years of rule

Akhenaten died after seventeen years of rule and was initially buried in a tomb in the Royal Wadi east of Akhet-Aten. The order to construct the tomb and to bury the pharaoh there was commemorated on one of the boundary stela delineating the capital's borders: "Let a tomb be made for me in the eastern mountain [of Akhet-Aten]. Let my burial be made in it, in the millions of jubilees which the Aten, my father, decreed for me." In the years following the burial, Akhenaten's sarcophagus was destroyed and left in the Akhet-Aten necropolis; reconstructed in the 20th century, it is in the Egyptian Museum in Cairo as of 2019. Despite leaving the sarcophagus behind, Akhenaten's mummy was removed from the royal tombs after Tutankhamun abandoned Akhet-Aten and returned to Thebes. It was most likely moved to tomb KV55 in the Valley of the Kings near Thebes. This tomb was later desecrated, likely during the Ramesside period.

Legacy

With Akhenaten's death, the Aten cult he had founded fell out of favour: at first gradually, and then with decisive finality. Tutankhaten changed his name to Tutankhamun in Year 2 of his reign (c. 1332 BCE) and abandoned the city of Akhet-Aten. Their successors then attempted to erase Akhenaten and his family from the historical record. During the reign of Horemheb, the last pharaoh of the Eighteenth Dynasty and the first pharaoh after Akhenaten who was not related to Akhenaten's family, Egyptians started to destroy temples to the Aten and reuse the building blocks in new construction projects, including in temples for the newly restored god Amun.

Horemheb's successor continued in this effort. Seti I restored monuments to Amun and had the god's name re-carved on inscriptions where it was removed by Akhenaten.

Seti I also ordered that Akhenaten, Smenkhkare, Neferneferuaten, Tutankhamun and Ay be excised from official lists of pharaohs to make it appear that Amenhotep III was immediately succeeded by Horemheb. Under the Ramessides, who succeeded Seti I, Akhet-Aten was gradually destroyed and the building material reused across the country, such as in constructions at Hermopolis. The negative attitudes toward Akhenaten were illustrated by, for example, inscriptions in the tomb of scribe Mose (or Mes), where Akhenaten's reign is referred to as "the time of the enemy of Akhet-Aten."

Atenism

Egyptians worshipped a sun god under several names, and solar worship had been growing in popularity even before Akhenaten, especially during the Eighteenth Dynasty and the reign of Amenhotep III, Akhenaten's father. During the New Kingdom, the pharaoh started to be associated with the sun disc; for example, one inscription called the pharaoh Hatshepsut the "female Re shining like the Disc", while Amenhotep III was described as "he who rises over every foreign land, Nebmare, the dazzling disc." During the Eighteenth Dynasty, a religious hymn to the sun also appeared and became popular among Egyptians. However, Egyptologists question whether there is a causal relationship between the cult of the sun disc before Akhenaten and his religious policies.

Implementation and development

By Year 9 of his reign, Akhenaten declared that Aten was not merely the supreme god, but the only worshipable god. He ordered the defacing of Amun's temples throughout Egypt and, in a number of instances, inscriptions of the plural 'gods' were also removed. This emphasized the changes encouraged by the new regime, which included a ban on images, with the exception of a rayed solar disc, in which the rays appear to represent the unseen spirit of Aten, who by then was evidently considered not merely a sun god, but rather a universal deity.

All life on Earth depended on the Aten and the visible sunlight. Representations of the Aten were always accompanied with a sort of hieroglyphic footnote, stating that the representation of the sun as all-encompassing creator was to be taken as just that: a representation of something that, by its very nature as something transcending creation, cannot be fully or adequately represented by any one part of that creation. Aten's name was also written differently starting as early as Year 8 or as late as Year 14, according to some historians. From "Living Re-Horakhty, who rejoices in the horizon in his name Shu-Re who is in Aten," the god's name changed to "Living Re, ruler of the horizon, who rejoices in his name of Re the father who has returned as Aten," removing the Aten's connection to Re-Horakhty and Shu, two other solar deities. The Aten thus became an amalgamation that incorporated the attributes and beliefs around Re-Horakhty, universal sun god, and Shu, god of the sky and manifestation of the sunlight.

Akhenaten's Atenist beliefs are best distilled in the Great Hymn to the Aten. The hymn was discovered in the tomb of Ay, one of Akhenaten's successors, though Egyptologists believe that it could have been composed by Akhenaten himself. The hymn celebrates

Pharaoh Akhenaten, Colossal statue from Karnak, Luxor Museum

the sun and daylight and recounts the dangers that abound when the sun sets. It tells of the Aten as a sole god and the creator of all life, who recreates life every day at sunrise, and on whom everything on Earth depends, including the natural world, people's lives, and even trade and commerce. In one passage, the hymn declares: "O Sole God beside whom there is none! You made the earth as you wished, you alone." The hymn also states that Akhenaten is the only intermediary between the god and Egyptians, and the only one who can understand the Aten: "You are in my heart, and there is none who knows you except your son."

Atenism and other gods

Some debate has focused on the extent to which Akhenaten forced his religious reforms on his people. Certainly, as time drew on, he revised the names of the Aten, and other religious language, to increasingly exclude references to other gods; at some point, also, he embarked on the wide-scale erasure of traditional gods' names, especially those of Amun. Some of his court changed their names to remove them from the patronage of other gods and place them under that of Aten (or Ra, with whom Akhenaten equated the Aten). Yet, even at Amarna itself, some courtiers kept such names as Ahmose ("child of the moon god", the owner of tomb 3), and the sculptor's workshop where the famous Nefertiti bust and other works of royal portraiture were found is associated with an artist known to have been called Thutmose ("child of Thoth"). An overwhelmingly large number of faience amulets at Amarna also show that talismans of the household-and-childbirth gods Bes and Taweret, the eye of Horus, and amulets of other traditional deities, were openly worn by its citizens. Indeed, a cache of royal jewellery found buried near the Amarna royal tombs (now in the National Museum of Scotland) includes a finger ring referring to Mut, the wife of Amun. Such evidence suggests that though Akhenaten shifted funding away from traditional temples, his policies were fairly tolerant until some point, perhaps a particular event as yet unknown, toward the end of the reign.

After Akhenaten

Following Akhenaten's death, Egypt gradually returned to its traditional polytheistic religion, partly because of how closely associated the Aten became with Akhenaten. Atenism likely stayed dominant through the reigns of Akhenaten's immediate successors, Smenkhkare and Neferneferuaten, as well as early in the reign of Tutankhaten. For some years the worship of Aten and a resurgent worship of Amun coexisted.

Artistic depictions

Styles of art that flourished during the reigns of Akhenaten and his immediate successors, known as Amarna art, are markedly different from the traditional art of ancient Egypt. Representations are more realistic, expressionistic, and naturalistic, especially in depictions of animals, plants and people, and convey more action and movement for both non-royal and royal individuals than the traditionally static representations. In traditional art, a pharaoh's divine nature was expressed by repose, even immobility.

The portrayals of Akhenaten himself greatly differ from the depictions of other pharaohs. Traditionally, the portrayal of pharaohs – and the Egyptian ruling class – was idealized, and they were shown in "stereotypically 'beautiful' fashion" as youthful and athletic. However, Akhenaten's portrayals are unconventional and "unflattering" with a sagging stomach; broad hips; thin legs; thick thighs; large, "almost feminine breasts;" a thin, "exaggeratedly long face;" and thick lips.

Speculative theories

There are strong similarities between Akhenaten's Great Hymn to the Aten and the Biblical Psalm 104, but there is debate as to the relationship implied by this similarity.

Others have likened some aspects of Akhenaten's relationship with the Aten to the relationship, in Christian tradition, between Jesus Christ and God, particularly interpretations that emphasize a more monotheistic interpretation of Atenism than a henotheistic one. Donald B. Redford has noted that some have viewed Akhenaten as a harbinger of Jesus. "After all, Akhenaten did call himself the son of the sole god: 'Thine only son that came forth from thy body'." James Henry Breasted likened him to Jesus, Arthur Weigall saw him as a failed precursor of Christ and Thomas Mann saw him "as right on the way and yet not the right one for the way".

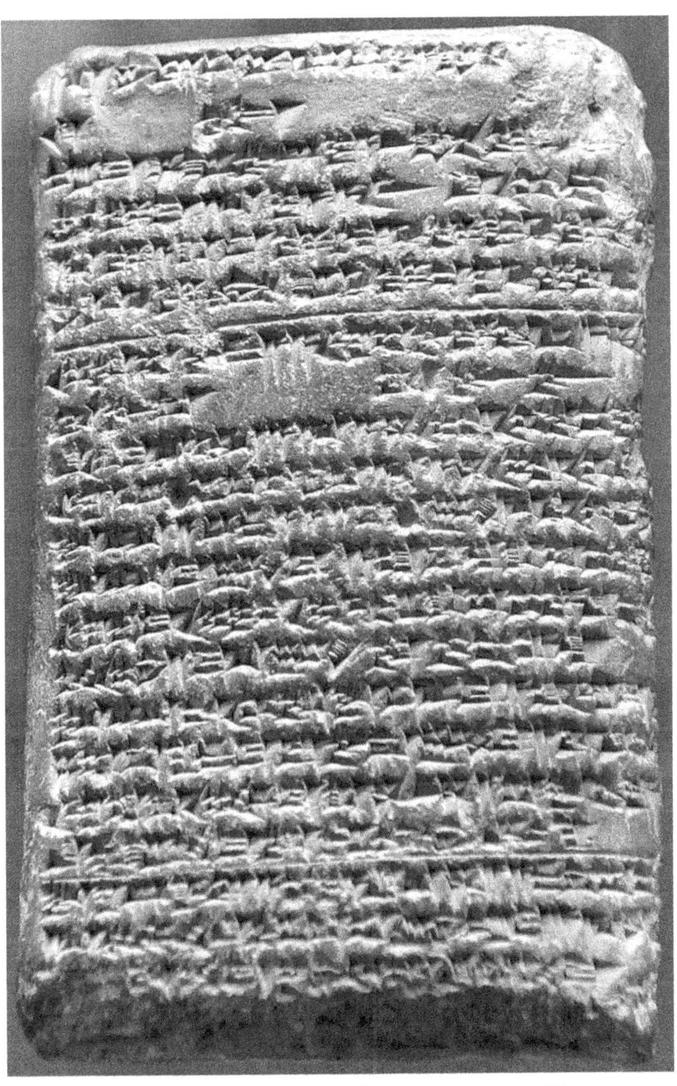

Cuneiform Amarna letter from the Assyrian King
Assur-uballit to Amunhotep IV

Great Temple of the Aten

The Great Temple of the Aten was a temple located in the city of el-Amarna (ancient Akhet-Aten), Egypt. It served as the main place of worship of the deity Aten during the reign of the 18th Dynasty pharaoh Akhenaten (c. 1353–1336 BCE). Akhenaten ushered in a unique period of ancient Egyptian history by establishing the new religious cult dedicated to the sun-disk Aten, originally an aspect of Ra, the sun god in traditional ancient Egyptian religion. The king shut down traditional worship of other deities like Amun-Ra, and brought in a new era, though short-lived, of seeming monotheism where the Aten was worshipped as a sun god and Akhenaten and his wife, Nefertiti, represented the divinely royal couple that connected the people with the god. Although he began construction at Karnak during his rule, the association the city had with other gods drove Akhenaten to establish a new city and capital at Amarna for the Aten. Akhenaten built the city along the east bank of the Nile River, setting up workshops, palaces, suburbs and temples. The Great Temple of the Aten was located just north of the Central City and, as the largest temple dedicated to the Aten, was where Akhenaten fully established the proper cult and worship of the sun-disk.

Construction of Akhet-Aten

The city of Akhet-Aten was built rather hastily and was constructed mostly of mud-brick. Mud-bricks were made by drying in the sun and they measured 33–37 cm x 15–16 cm x 9–10 cm, although bricks for temple enclosure walls were slightly larger, at 38

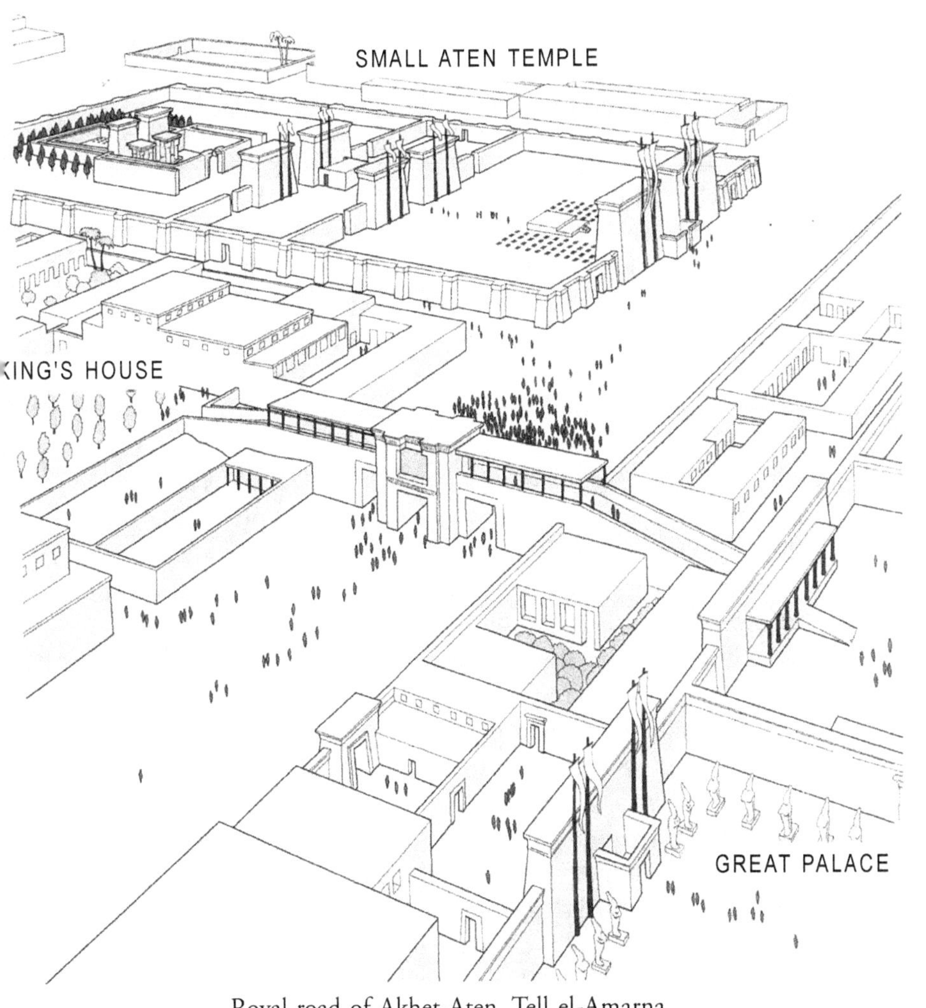

Royal road of Akhet-Aten, Tell el-Amarna

cm x 16 cm x 16 cm. During construction, bricks were laid down with a small amount of mortar between the rows and no mortar between adjacent bricks. There was no rain to deteriorate the bricks but they would wear down from wind-swept sand, so for protection walls were plastered with a layer of mud that could be reapplied. As the bricks dried, they often shrank leading to warping and structural problems, so a technique was developed of arranging the rows of bricks so that every other row was nearly hollow, allowing for air to circulate. While this helped walls keep their form, it also acted to weaken the walls so particularly high constructions meant to hold a lot of weight had to be made differently. For pylon towers and large surrounding walls like those at the Great Temple of the Aten, timber was used for structural support and the public buildings within the Temple had stone columns and were built of other stones for more support. Stone columns conformed to the usual style found elsewhere in Egypt, representing either palm-frond or papyrus. To lay out structural elements like offering tables and pits on a plaster floor, string was used. The string was first dipped in black paint and stretched tightly and was allowed to touch the ground, leaving a mark. In some instances the string was even pushed into the plaster floor, leaving a shallow groove. A similar technique was used to divide up wall surfaces before they were decorated with relief.

The actual construction of the temple was accomplished in a series of steps. Before anything was built, there was already some kind of dedication ceremony at the site. A ceremonial gateway with receptacles for liquid offerings stood at the beginning of a paved avenue. The avenue extended eastward and was lined with sphinxes, but they were later replaced by trees (tree pits, some still containing tree roots, have been excavated). The avenue led up to a small mud-brick shrine which was later built into the main design scheme of the Temple. The first main construction undertaken by Akhenaten was the building of the temenos wall, enclosing a huge area of 229m x 730m. As the wall was being completed, the stone Sanctuary at the east end of the enclosure was built. This Sanctuary seemed to function on its own for some time until a few years later when Akhenaten added the Gem-Aten on the west side of the enclosure. With this addition, the original ceremonial gate had to be taken down and a raised causeway was built over it. The Gem-Aten was originally constructed in stone, but it seems that as time went on Akhenaten ran low on materials and the latter part of the Gem-Aten was finished with mud-brick. It is unknown exactly how the Temple walls were decorated because the entire area was destroyed later on, but fragments that have been found show that there were many statues of Akhenaten and his family placed all around the Temple.

Layout of Akhet-Aten

The Great Temple of the Aten lay to the north of the Central City part of Akhet-Aten and was separated from the Palace by many storehouses. The Temple was oriented on an east-west axis and the western entrance to the Great Temple was along the Royal Road, a road that ran through the city and parallel to the Nile River. Soon after the death of Akhenaten, Atenism was rejected as a religion and the city was destroyed. The temple was dismantled, covered in new sand, and paved over, but ironically this has preserved the site better than it might normally have been for archaeologists today. In 1890, Flinders Petrie, with permission from the Egyptian Antiquities Service, began excavating the area. Based on the remaining foundations he found, as well as on multiple scenes of the Great Temple found in private tomb decoration in Amarna, a comprehensive reconstruction of the temple has been possible.

One of the most distinctive aspects of the Temple was that there was no cult image of the god. Instead, the Temple was open-aired and had no roof, so that people worshipped the actual sun directly overhead as it traveled from east to west. In fact this was a common theme amongst all of the Aten temples; they were all arranged to direct worship towards the sky (such as in the Ḥwt Aten (Mansion of Aten), the smaller temple of Aten located 500m south of the Great Temple in Akhet-Aten).

In the Great Temple there were two main structures, the Gem-Aten and the Sanctuary, which were separated by about 300m. Upon entering the enclosure wall, one faced the first of these structures, the Gem-Aten, which was a very long building preceded by a court called the Per-Hai (House of Rejoicing). On the left of the main entrance to the Temple was a columned pavilion and on both the left and the right were small chapels. These chapels, originally built for Queen Kiya, were later taken over by the elder princesses. The first great pylon directly ahead was the entrance into the Per-Hai and it had swinging doors and five pairs of tall masts with crimson pennants flanking the doorway. The inside of the Per-Hai had two rows of four columns on each side. Within these colonnades were altars made of limestone carved with images of the King and Queen giving offerings. Through the Per-Hai and the next great pylon was the Gem-Aten, the [Place of] He Who Found the Aten, and this was a series of six courtyards separated by pylons, all leading to a main sanctuary and altar. This Temple differed from temples of other gods because as one progressed through the courts, they became more open to the air and light, as opposed to temples like those of Amun-Ra where the halls would get darker

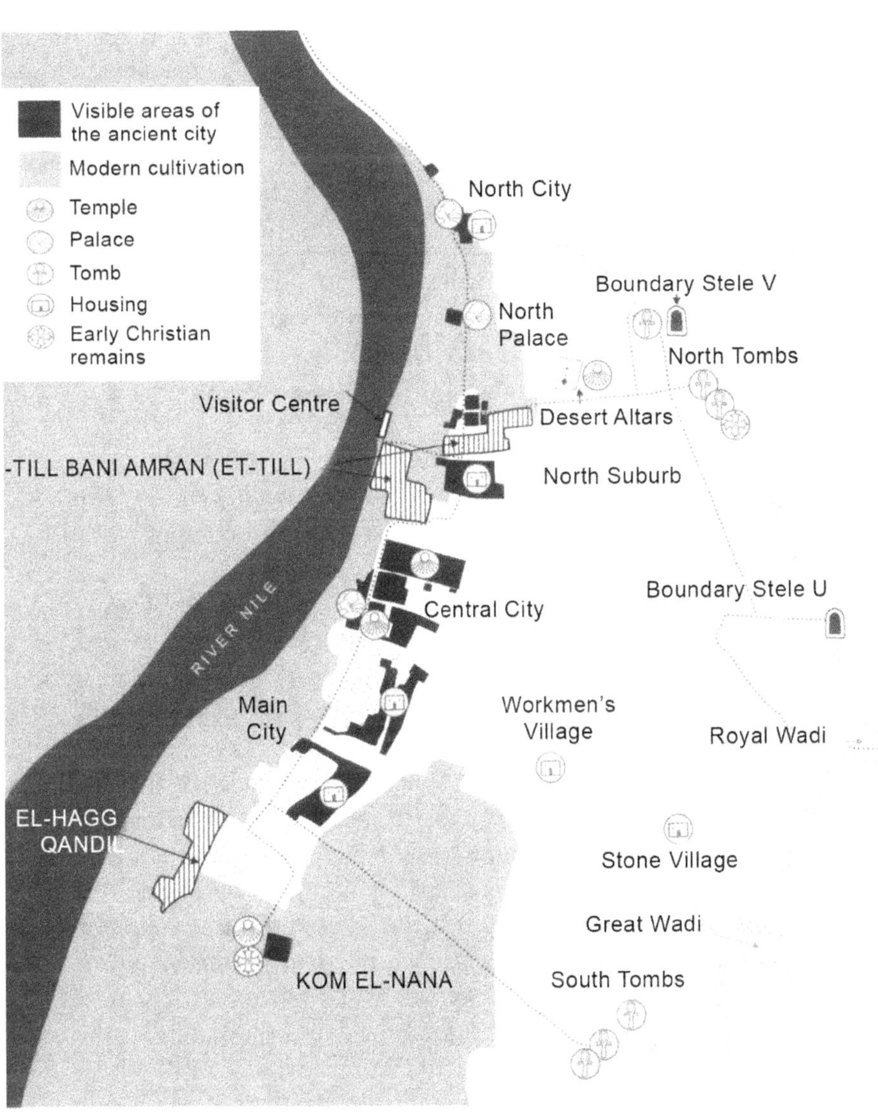

Map of Akhet-Aten, Tell el-Amarna

and more shrouded in mystery. The first court had a high altar with small chapels and chambers on either side. Each successive court had altars and magazines where offering supplies could be stored. The fourth court was columned and had many furnished chambers where people could rest in the shade. The final court had a main High Altar intended for the Royal pair, and it was surrounded by 365 mud-brick altars on either side, one for each day of the year, divided to represent Upper and Lower Egypt. The offerings given here were dedicated to the Aten but were then used to feed the officiating priests, the temple staff, and even some of the local populace. Beyond this High Altar the Gem-Aten abruptly ended in a blank wall, which shows no sign of having had a door in it. On the outside of the Gem-Aten there was enough room to have a large ambulatory and there were 40 rows of 20 offering tables set up on each side.

Between the Gem-Aten and the Sanctuary, the main building at the east end of the enclosure, was a smaller, more sacred pillared portico with statues of the pharaoh Akhenaten and his family standing in front of each column. Inside the portico was a great quartzite stela next to a colossal seated statue of Akhenaten. This stela was carved with images of Akhenaten and Nefertiti and was a variation of a benben stone, a sacred solar symbol of Heliopolis. Traditionally, the benben stone was a representation of the island created by the sun-god Atum at the beginning of the world. This marked one of the holiest areas in the Temple and it was heaped in flowers and offerings. Today only a fragment of this stone has been found (discovered by Carter in 1892), but it was identified as a benben stone based on scenes of the Temple found in nearby tombs.

Also between the Gem-Aten and the Sanctuary in the Great Temple was a large square building where meat offerings were

The remains of Mansion of Aten in Akhet-Aten, Tell el-Amarna
Coordinates 27⁰ 38' 43.58" N, 30⁰ 53' 44.30" E

They built a brand new city called Akhet-Aten in the exact centre of Egypt. We still don't know how they got it in the exact centre. Akhenaten put a stone there that says, "This is the centre of the country." Today we could not have done it better from a satellite. It makes you wonder who these people were who could locate right down to the square inch the centre of a country hundreds of miles long. It's pretty amazing. They built an entire city out of white stones. It was beautiful - it was space-age.

Drunvalo Melchizedek

slaughtered and prepared, but further excavation of the area is difficult because of the presence of the modern-day cemetery of Et-Till.

The second main structure of the Great Temple was the Sanctuary at its east end, which may have been inspired by the Fifth Dynasty Sun Temples at Abu Ghuroub (c. 2400 BCE). The Sanctuary started with a pylon that led into an open court, on the south side of which were three houses probably intended for the priests on duty. A second pylon led to a causeway that went through two large colonnades with colossal statues of Akhenaten on either side wearing the Red Crown and the White Crown. The causeway continued into a final court that had a high altar surrounded by offering tables. This main altar was probably intended just for the Royal Family, especially after the Gem-Aten was built and put into regular use. Behind the Sanctuary there were other rooms including a large room which housed the original shrine of the dedication ceremony, but these rooms were only accessible from outside the Sanctuary.

Against the north-eastern end of the enclosure wall was one final altar called the Hall of Foreign Tribute. This was a large set-in altar and was most likely where offerings from foreign lands were made.

View of Akhet-Aten, Tell el-Amarna, from the Boundary Stela U

The Boundary Stelae of Akhet-Aten

The sacred territory of Akhetaten comprised an arc of desert on the east of the Nile bounded by tall cliffs, a broad tract of agricultural land with villages across the river on the west, and a narrower strip of western desert in front of a low escarpment.

The whole tract of land measured around 20-25 kilometres across the valley by 13 kilometres from south to north. It was marked out by a series of tablets or stelae carved into the cliffs and escarpment on both sides. In modern times they have become known as the Amarna Boundary Stelae. Each one is a rectangle with a rounded top sculpted from the rock. The main rectangular part was carved with many horizontal lines of hieroglyphic text; a picture of the royal family worshipping the Aten filled the rounded top panel. Most of the stelae were accompanied by statues of Akhenaten and Nefertiti and some of their daughters, also carved from the rock.

The main text on each stela contains one or other of two proclamations made by Akhenaten, the first in the fifth year of his reign, the second in his sixth year (with an added reaffirmation in his eighth year). The first proclamation is found on stelae K, M and X; the second is found on stelae A, B, F (thus all three on the west side), J, N, P, Q, R, S, U and V. Stela L is a small rectangular tablet, beside stela M, without pictures or statues that seems to give an abbreviated version of one of the proclamations. Stela H, with a statue group, was carved into rock so poor that any hieroglyphic text is likely to have been cut into an added layer of gypsum plaster, now vanished. When freshly cut they would have been a dazzling white (perhaps muted somewhat by having been

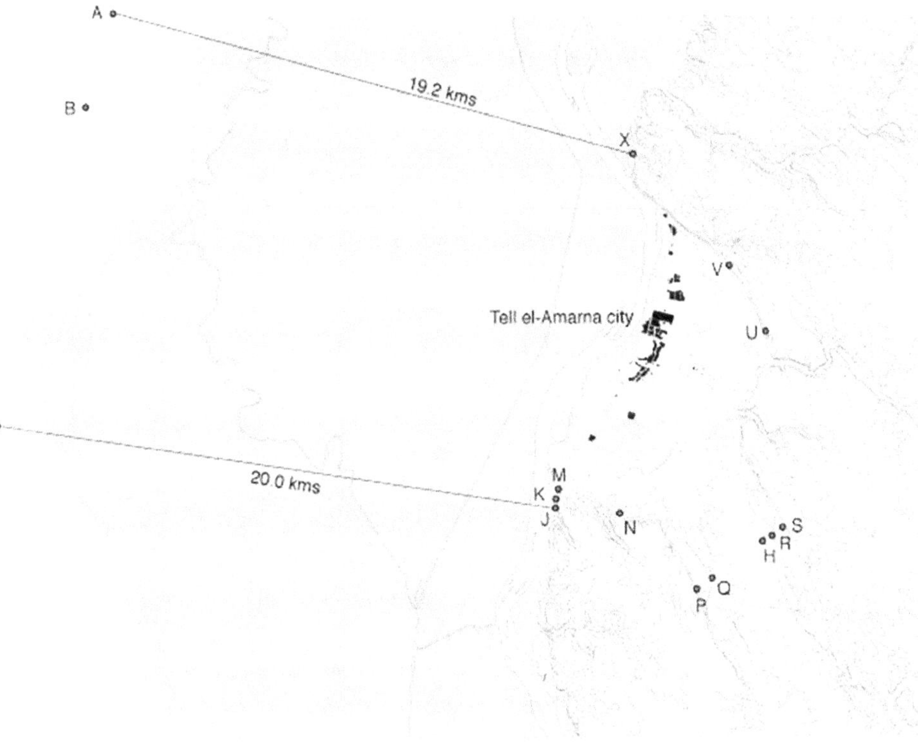

Map of Boundary Stelae in Akhet-Aten, Tell el-Amarna

partially painted) and visible from afar. It was also intended that they would be visited, for broad paths made by clearing stones to each side ran up to several of them.

The texts of both proclamations are long, repetitive and also damaged and partially untranslatable as a result, especially towards the end. In the first proclamation Akhenaten sets out his intentions. It is dated to his regnal year 5, 4th month of winter, day 13 :

'On this day, when One (Pharaoh Akhenaten) was in Akhetaten, His Majesty [appeared] on the great chariot of electrum... Setting [off] on a good road [toward] Akhetaten, His place of creation, which He made for Himself that He might set within it every day... There was presented a great offering to the Father, The Aten, consisting of bread, beer, long- and short-horned cattle, calves, fowl, wine, fruits, incense, all kinds of fresh green plants, and everything good, in front of the mountain of Akhetaten...'

The king addresses his gathered courtiers:

'As the Aten is beheld, the Aten desires that there be made for him [...] as a monument with an eternal and everlasting name. Now, it is the Aten, my father, who advised me concerning it, [namely] Akhetaten. No official has ever advised me concerning it, not any of the people who are in the entire land has ever advised me concerning it, to suggest making Akhetaten in this distant place. It was the Aten, my father, who advised me concerning it, so that it might be made for Him as Akhetaten... Behold, it is Pharaoh who has discovered it: not being the property of a god, not being the property of a goddess, not being the property of a ruler, not being the property of a female ruler, not being the property of any people to lay claim to it....'

'I shall make Akhetaten for the Aten, my father, in this place. I shall not make Akhetaten for him to the south of it, to the north of it, to the west of it, to the east of it. I shall not expand beyond the southern stela of Akhetaten toward the south, nor shall I expand beyond the northern stela of Akhetaten toward the north, in order to make Akhetaten for him there. Nor shall I make (it) for him on the western side of Akhetaten, but I shall make Akhetaten for the Aten, my father, on the east of Akhetaten, the place which He Himself made to be enclosed for Him by the mountain...'

'I shall make the "House of the Aten" for the Aten, my father, in Akhetaten in this place. I shall make the "Mansion of the Aten" for

Boundary Stela U at Akhet-Aten, Tell el-Amarna

Boundary Stela N, Akhet-Aten, Tell el-Amarna

Reconstruction of the original appearance of Boundary Stela N

the Aten, my father, in Akhetaten in this place. I shall make the Sun Temple of the [Great King's] Wife [Nefernefruaten-Nefertiti] for the Aten, my father, in Akhetaten in this place. I shall make the "House of Rejoicing" for the Aten, my father, in the "Island of the Aten, Distinguished in Jubilees" in Akhetaten in this place... I shall make for myself the apartments of Pharaoh, I shall make the apartments of the Great King's Wife in Akhetaten in this place.'

'Let a tomb be made for me in the eastern mountain of Akhetaten. Let my burial be made in it, in the millions of jubilees which the Aten, my father, has decreed for me. Let the burial of the Great King's Wife, Nefertiti, be made in it, in the millions of yea[rs which the Aten, my father, decreed for her. Let the burial of] the King's Daughter, Meritaten, [be made] in it, in these millions of years. If I die in any town downstream, to the south, to the west, to the east in these millions of years, let me be brought back, that I may be buried in Akhetaten. If the Great King's Wife, Nefertiti, dies in any town downstream, to the south, to the west, to the east in these millions of years, let her be brought back, that she may be buried in Akhetaten. If the King's Daughter, Meritaten, dies in any town downstream, to the south, to the west, to the east in the millions of years, let her be brought back, that she may be buried in Akhetaten. Let a cemetery for the Mnevis Bull [be made] in the eastern mountain of Akhetaten, that he may be buried in it. Let the tombs of the Chief of Seers, of the God's Fathers of the [Aten.......] be made in the eastern mountain of Akhetaten, that they may be buried in it. Let [the tombs] of the priests of the [Aten] be [made in the eastern mountain of Akhetaten] that they may b[e bur]ied in it'.

The second proclamation was mainly concerned with fixing even more securely the limits of Akhetaten and with dedicating all the enclosed land to the Aten. The stelae have sometimes been mistakenly interpreted as saying that Akhenaten himself intended

Boundary Stela R, Akhet-Aten, Tell el-Amarna

never to leave Akhetaten, whereas the injunction is against extending the limits of the territory. The stated arrangements for his burial show that he envisaged travelling outside it.

The stelae and their accompanying statues have suffered various degrees of natural erosion and human damage, some of it quite recent. Davies noted in his 1908 publication: 'Stela P was blown to pieces by gunpowder a few years ago by Copts, who expected, as all Egyptians do, to find that the stela was a door to a hidden treasure-chamber'. The best preserved in his day was Stela S, on which he remarked : 'The sculptors chanced on a vein of limestone as hard as alabaster, so that the greater part of the monument is marvellously preserved, though spiteful attacks have been made upon it lately'. Most subsequent attacks on the stelae involved cutting deep and wide grooves across them to assist in the removal of irregular slabs which could then be sold to collectors and museums. Thus pieces of Stela R were bought in the 1940s by the Louvre in Paris. A 1984 photograph of Stela S shows the face of this most admired of stelae ravaged in this way. Early in 2004, however, the earlier manner of destruction was returned to, and the entire stela and its statues were blown out of the hillside with quarry explosives. Many of the pieces were subsequently collected by the local inspectorate of the Supreme Council of Antiquities with a view to restoring it.

Drawing of the top part of the Boundary Stela S
Akhet-Aten, Tell el-Amarna,

Worship of Aten

In hieroglyphic inscriptions, on the royal cartouches, and on the entranceways of temples, the winged sun circle appears throughout Egyptian architecture. In Egypt it was originally a pair of falcon wings symbolizing the ethereal, but during the fifth dynasty two serpents and a sun disk were inserted between the wings, representing Horus of Behdet.

The cult of the Aten was celebrated daily and was very simple. Although there were other priests, Akhenaten acted as his own High Priest and special roles were given to the royal women. Since there was no cult statue, the traditional acts of raising and washing the god played no role in the Great Temple and worship rather consisted solely of singing hymns and giving offerings to the Aten.

Some hymns told stories, such as one that attributed the Aten with the creation of the human race and recognized that people were created differently, to speak different languages and have different coloured skins, while other hymns simply expressed adoration and gratitude to the Aten.

Akhenaten, Nefertiti and their eldest daughter workshiping the Aten, both are shown in the early Amarna, exaggerated style.

Offerings consisted of food, drink, flowers and perfume and were often accompanied by burning incense and pouring libations. To consecrate offerings, a special baton called a *ḥrp* was used to touch the offerings, marking them as meant for the Aten.

Each day, the royal family approached the temple on chariots after riding up and down the Royal Road, and entered the temple precinct and presented offerings in front of the Gem-Aten. The king and queen then consecrated their offerings with the *ḥrp* while their daughters rattled sistra. The family then passed through the pylons of the Gem-Aten and mounted the steps of the High Altar where there were offerings of meat, poultry, vegetables, and flowers already laid out and surmounted by three pans of burning incense.

As the king and queen officiated, priests then placed offerings on many of the other altars for the public people while music was played. The princesses continued to rattle the sistra while four male chanters sang hymns to the Aten within the Gem-Aten court.

Outside the Gem-Aten were female musicians who performed along with the temple choir which was made up of blind singers and a blind harpist. These musicians performed at intervals throughout the day and were never allowed beyond the outer court.

King Akhenaten and the Queen Nefertiti, workshiping the Aten
Egyptian Museum, Cairo

The Great Hymn to the Aten

The Great Hymn to the Aten is the longest of a number of hymn-poems written to the sun-disk deity Aten. Composed in the middle of the 14th century BCE, it is varyingly attributed to the 18th Dynasty Pharaoh Akhenaten or his courtiers, depending on the version, who radically changed traditional forms of Egyptian religion by replacing them with Atenism.

The hymn-poem provides a glimpse of the religious artistry of the Amarna period expressed in multiple forms encompassing literature, new temples, and in the building of a whole new city at the site of present-day Amarna as the capital of Egypt. Egyptologist Toby Wilkinson said that "It has been called 'one of the most significant and splendid pieces of poetry to survive from the pre Homeric world.'" Egyptologist John Darnell asserts that the hymn was sung.

Various courtiers' rock tombs at Amarna (ancient Akhet-Aten) have similar prayers or hymns to the deity Aten or to the Aten and Akhenaten jointly. One of these, found in almost identical form in five tombs, is known as The Short Hymn to the Aten. The long version discussed in this article was found in the tomb of the courtier (and later Pharaoh) Ay.

The 18th Dynasty Pharaoh Akhenaten forbade the worship of other gods, a radical departure from the centuries of Egyptian religious practice. Akhenaten's religious reforms (later regarded as heretical and reversed under his successor Pharaoh Tutankhamun) have been described by some scholars as monotheistic, though others consider them to be henotheistic.

These particular excerpts are not attributed to Aten himself; this long version was found in the tomb of the courtier Ay.
From the middle of the text:

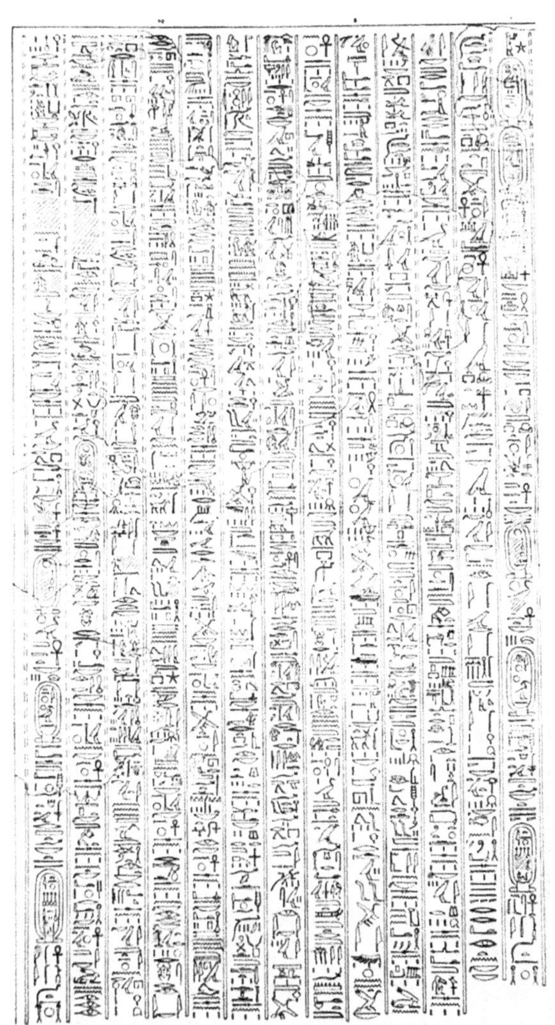

Carved in its most complete version in the Amarna tomb of the official Ay. The great Hymn to Atenis one of the world's outstanding examples of religious literature.

The great Hymn to Aten

May you appear beautiful in the horizon of heaven,
*   O living Aten, who creates life,*
*   You having arisen in the eastern horizon.*
You have filled every land with your perfection.
You are beautiful, great, dazzling, high over every country.
Your rays fall on the lands, to the limit of all that you have created,
*   You are Re, you have reached the last limits*
*   When you subdue them for the son whom you love.*
You are far away, but your rays fall on the earth,
*   You are visible, but your movements are never seen.*

✺

When you go to rest in the western horizon
*   The land is in darkness in a state of death.*
The sleepers are in their bedchambers
*   Their heads covered by darkness,*
*   Not one eye can see the other,*
*   If all they possess gets stolen*
*   Which is hidden under their sleeping heads*
*   They will not feel it.*
Every lion has come out from his cave
*   All worms and snakes, sting and bite.*
Dark is the fireplace, the land is silent.
*   As long the one who made all has gone to rest behind the horizon.*

✺

The great Hymn to the Aten in the South Tomb 25 - Ay and his wife,
God's father, Fan-bearer on the Right Hand of the King,
Overseer of horses of His Majesty.

But, with you rising again on the horizon
    And shining as the sun disk during the day,
    You have driven away the darkness
    And you have sent out your sunrays.
The two lands are in festival
    The sun-folk having awakened and stand on their feet.
You have lifted them up
    Their bodies are cleaned, putting on their festive clothes
    Their arms are arisen in adoration
    While you appear in glory,
    The entire land carries out their work.
All cattle are content with their fodder
    The trees and plants flourish.
Birds are flying from their nests
    Their wings in praise of your Ka-spirit!

All small flocks leap up on their feet,
    All that flies and flutters is alive,
    After you have arisen for them.
Ships go north and south likewise,
    Every road is open because you appear in glory.
    The fish in the river leap up in front of your face,
    Your rays are reaching deep into the sea.

✸

You are the One who makes the fetus develop in a woman,
    Who transforms water into humans,
    Who enlivens the son in the womb of his mother.
Who quiets him with love which will stop his tears.
    Nurse in the womb, you give the breath,

The one who gives life to all that he has created!
  When the son starts breathing on the day of his birth,
  It is you who opens his mouth and cares for his needs.

The chick in the egg peeps from his shell
  Because you give him the air to breath.
After you fixed the time to break from his shell,
  He comes out of the egg and peeps,
  Then he comes out of the egg and starts to walk on two legs.

How many are your deeds,
  Although they are hidden from our sight.
  The only god with no other beside him.
You created the earth according to your wish, you are alone,
  While all people, cattle and small flocks,
  Everything on earth that stands on their feet,
  All that flies in heaven, around on their wings.

Also the foreign lands of Syria, Kush, which belong to Egypt,
  You set every man in his proper place and you look to his needs
  Each one has his requirements and you calculated his lifetime.
Their tongues are in different languages, their natures likewise.
  Their skin is different, for you to identify the foreigners.

✳

You create the Nile in the Underworld
  And you bring out of it as much as you wanted,
  to keep the people alive, just as you have created them.
You are their lord entirely, wearied by means of them.
  The lord of every land, who shines for them,
  The sun disk during the day, the great One in Wonder.

Also for all in distant foreign lands, you make them alive.
*   Because you have set a Nile in the sky*
*   So that he can descend on them,*
*   That he makes waves on the mountains, like the sea,*
*   To water their fields with so much as needed.*
*   How successful are your plans, O lord of eternity!*

Because the Nile in heaven is made for all the people in foreign countries
For all the mountain wildlife running on legs,
But the Nile which comes from the deep underground is there for Egypt.

Your rays nurture all plants.
*   As you rise so they live and grow for you.*
You make the seasons, to create all that is created.
*   The wintertime is there for cooling,*
*   The summer heat so that they might experience you.*

✳

You have made the far heaven, in order to rise on it
*   And to see all that you have made*
*   You being alone and risen in your transformations as living Aten*
*   You having appeared in glory*
*   You are shining, you being far yet near.*
*   Out from yourself you make millions of manifestations only one.*
*   You create millions of shapes out of yourself:*
*   Cities, villages and fields, roads and rivers.*
*   All eyes can see you, very clear,*
*   During the day when the sun disk stands high in the sky.*
You are moving in the presence of each eye,

You are creating their field of vision,
  So that you make it perfect,
  The view of your body, that is yourself.

✶

O sole god. My action is for you,
Because you are in my heart!
Nobody knows you except your son,
  Whom you inform about all your intentions,
And about all your might you present.
  The earth is created by your hands,
  Exactly as you conceive all your creatures.
After you rising they will live. When you go down, they will die.
  You are yourself the lifetime, because of you we are living.
The eyes exist, because of your beauty, until you go down;
All work stops, when you go down upon the western side.
But your rising strengthens the King
  Everyone who hurries by foot,
  Since you founded the land –
You raise them up for your son,
  Who comes forth from your flesh:
  The King of Upper and Lower Egypt,
  Who lives on maat, Lord of the Two Lands
  Neferkheperure, Unique One of Re;
  Son of Re who lives on maat,
  Lord of glorious appearances,
Akhenaten, great in his lifetime.
  The King's great wife, his beloved lady of the Two Lands,
  Nefernefernaten Nefertiti,
  May she live and be youthful for ever and ever.

What Really Happened to Akhenaten?

Most of Egypt hated Akhenaten, except for a small group. The priesthood hated him most of all because Egyptian religious beliefs were centred on the priests. They controlled the people, their way of life and the economy. They became rich and were more powerful than anybody else. Then Akhenaten came along and said, "You don't need priests; God is within you. There is only one God, and you can access God from within your own self." The priests reacted to protect themselves and their vested interests.

Also, Egypt had the most powerful military in the world, and when Akhenaten became pharaoh, they were chomping at the bit, ready to go out and take over the world. Akhenaten said no. He was a complete pacifist and said, "Come back onto our soil. Do not attack anyone unless you are attacked." He made the military come back and sit by idly, and they didn't like that.

So he had not only the priesthood, but the military against him. On top of that, the people themselves were into their little religions, and they loved worshiping their little gods. This wouldn't ultimately do them any good - it wouldn't get them where they needed to go according to the DNA plan of the universe which was back bone to God, to the one God but nevertheless they were really into what they were doing.

When the people were forcefully told that they could no longer do certain religious acts, this caused great animosity toward Akhenaten. It would be like our president saying, "Okay, there are no more religions in the United States; there's just the president's religion." And if the president brought all the military back onto American soil with an isolationist point of view, he wouldn't be very popular. Neither was Akhenaten. But he knew that he had to do it no matter what, even if it meant his own death.

He had to do it to correct the pathway that our collective DNA had encoded into the Reality. In addition, he needed to put into the akashic records the memory of the sacred purpose that Christ consciousness held. ...

Drunvalo Melchizedek
The Ancient Secret of the Flower of Life

Painting in the "Green Room" of the North Place, Akhet-Aten

The Royal Couple, Akhenaten and Nefertifi, at the palace balcony, or
Window of Appearance, with their three eldest daughters handing out
gifts to their followers.

Akhenaten and the Reign of Truth

Besides making the religions monotheistic again, Akhenaten also said, "In this new religion we're not going to have any more lying, no more untruthfulness. And we're going to change our art so that it reflects the total truth." So during the Eighteenth Dynasty - never before nor after - there was a totally unique art form. The artists were instructed to sculpt or paint things just as their eyes saw it, like a photograph. So began an art that looked realistic instead of stylized, as it had been before. You see ducks that look like ducks, just like we see in modern art. This is important to remember when you're looking at art of the Eighteenth Dynasty, because that means that whatever you see is exactly what the artist saw. They were not allowed to lie.

Drunvalo Melchizedek
The Ancient Secret of the Flower of Life, Vol. 1

Sculpture of Akhenaten and Nefertiti's daughter,
found in the Amarna workshop of the Royal Artisan Thutmose.

Akhenaten's Mystery School

What's important here is one fact: Akhenaten developed a mystery school. The school was called the Egyptian Mystery School of Akhenaten, the Law of One. As it turned out, he had only 17½ years to produce results.

He brought students from the Left Eye of Horus (the feminine side) Mystery School, which I'll talk about later - graduates who were at least 45 years old - into the Right Eye of Horus Mystery School. This right-eye information had never been taught before in Egypt. He taught them for twelve years, after which he had only five and a half years to see if he could get them to live immortality. And he did it! He got about 300 people into immortality. I believe they were all, or almost all, women.

Someone once asked, "Why didn't Akhenaten work with the population in a different way so as to not get himself into such a dangerous situation?" But can you think of a way to change a whole population in such a short time without causing strife? Could you do that in the United States right now - in one year bring all religions into one? I don't think there is a way except to just do it, even if it means getting "killed". Besides, the only thing he really needed to do was simply live his life. It would get into the akashic records and be a memory that we all have in our DNA.

One day alone would get it encoded, then afterwards they could do whatever they wanted with him. He wasn't really concerned about it. He knew that the country, the society and the customs would all go back to the old way. But he did have these 300 immortal people who would go on beyond him and Egypt.

Drunvalo Melchizedek
The Ancient Secret of the Flower of Life

Family tree of the Royal House of Akhet-Aten (Tell el-Amarna)

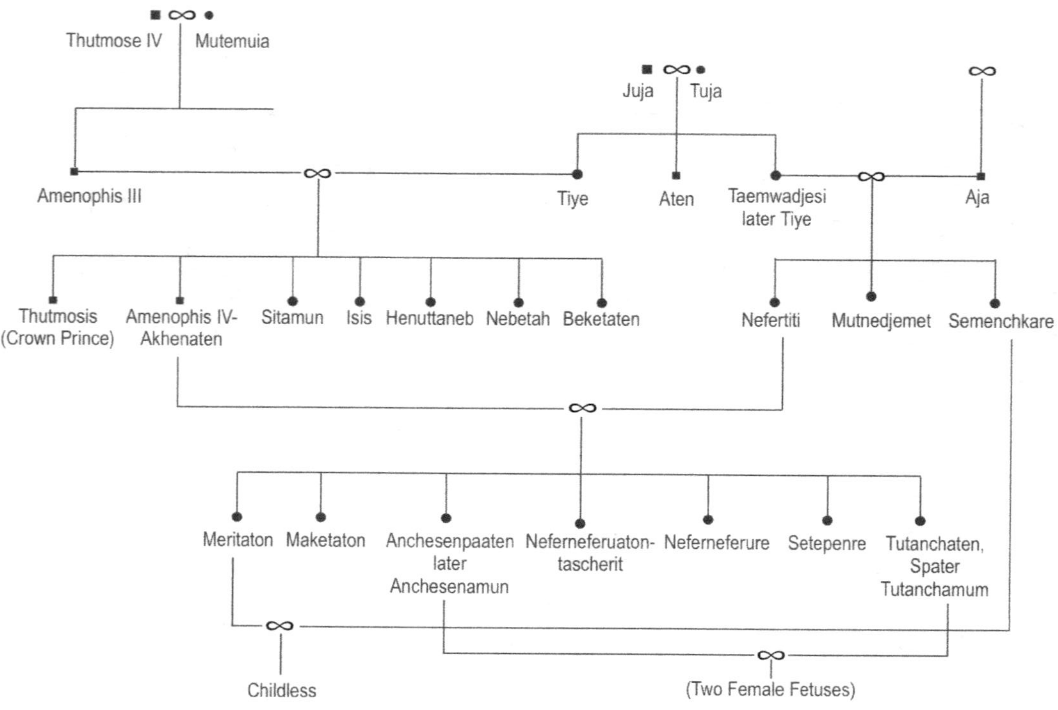

Sketch of Mira Ismalun, Mirra's grandmother by Mira Alfassa

Mira Ismalun

Little Mirra's (with two r's) grandmother was quite a character. There was something very sparkling and beguiling in Mira (with one r) Ismalun. And Mother had her own share of it.

Mira Ismalun was born in Cairo in 1830, on December 18.

But the Ismaluns had also some roots in the old Ural-Altaic region of Hungary, and Mira Ismalun's father, Said Pinto, although Egyptian, traced back his roots to Spain. Protean winds blew over little Mirra's cradle, those from the Urals mingling with the mysteries of the Valley of the Kings and the fiery Iberia. Mother has many roots, very ancient roots, and perhaps extending everywhere. "I am millions of years old, and I am waiting," she said during these last years, with a look in her eyes that seemed to carry the burden of the world and all the resistances of her earthly children. It reminds us of Walter Pater's moving study on Mona Lisa, with whom Mother had strange affinities and shared a certain smile: "She is older than the rocks among which she sits . . . she has been dead many times and learned the secret of the grave...."[1]

1830, Mehemet Ali is Viceroy of Egypt. The Suez Canal has not yet been dug. The Pasha's armies are rebelling against the yoke of the Ottoman Empire. A feudalistic Egypt confronts the modern world while still remembering Bonaparte. But Bonaparte's tempest had possibly left something in the air, for Mira Ismalun, too, lost no time in casting off the iron collar.

At the age of thirteen, in the wise and well-bred fashion of those days, she married a banker, after meeting her fiancé on a boat on the

---

1   Walter Pater, *The Renaissance Studies in Art Poetry* (Macmillan)

Nile. "He offered me a diadem of great value and a little basket of strawberries," she recounts in her memoirs, as delightful and funny as they are brief, which she dictated in French to her grandson, Governor Alfassa, when she was seventy-six years old. Our guess is that she appreciated the strawberries more than the diadem.

At the age of twenty she embarked for Italy, a daring act if we recall the situation of women in the Middle East more than a century ago. "I spoke only Arabic, wore my Egyptian dress and travelled alone with my two children and a governess, while my husband remained in Egypt. I was the first Egyptian woman to venture out of Egypt in this manner. ... I was found positively ravishing," she notes all the same, "in my sky-blue Egyptian robe, embroidered all over with gold and real pearls." She also sported a "small tarboosh worn very low, with a big gold tassel. . . . But I didn't know the language, so I vowed to learn it quickly." Which she did, and French too, for this lady was decidedly unusual, indeed a personage.

She made the acquaintance of the Grand Duke, "who sent me flowers every day, as did Rossini, the composer. But although well-bred and even strict," she adds with ingenuity, coquetry blending with wit, "I was not insensitive to all these attentions."

As for her strictness, we don't know. But we do know how exceptionally well she understood life, loved it frankly, and was endowed with a very universal spirit for which narrow patriotic frontiers seemed a vain and cumbersome contrivance.

She sent her eldest son to a boarding school in Vienna, herself commuting between Cairo and Europe, and later dropped off a second, then a third, son at *College Chaptal* in Paris. "I was wild about Paris. My temperament and character being original, it seemed to me quite permissible to go about everywhere only with

Elvire [her eldest daughter]. But as my attire was very elegant and rather conspicuous, wherever I went I attracted a great deal of attention."

But the attention was not due to her dress and her looks alone. For Mira Ismalun was no featherbrain. She read Renan, Taine, Nietzsche, Darwin. She was also endowed with a remarkable poise (exactly like Mother) and knew how to reconcile opposites: "One of my most consistent character traits has been to keep the head and the heart in a constant, reciprocal equilibrium, thus avoiding getting involved in the excesses of either.

... As for my finances, I took great care to balance my income with my expenditures." Finding out that back in Egypt the princesses in their harems were dying to know about Parisian life, she had the brilliant idea of combining the useful with the agreeable, and packed her suitcases with the latest creations from *Worth*, jewellery from Rue de la Paix, perfumes and chronicles thus defraying the expenses of her own extravagances. "Everywhere I went, I was hailed and catered to like a queen. My dignified air, my strict comportment, my stunning wardrobe and my lavish expenditures placed me on a veritable pedestal."

She also brought back oil-paintings; for the little princesses were very eager to see their own portraits, with their full array of jewellery, faithful reproductions of their photographs by the finest Parisian artists. So it was that Mira Ismalun mingled with the *Tout-Paris*, the Paris of the artists and the atelier of Vienot and Edouard Morisset, who was to become the father of young Mirra's husband.

Mira Ismalun's understanding of life made her liberal-minded. She had little concern for narrow patriotic frontiers, nor did she allow herself to get bogged down in religion. She let her children pursue freely their own separate ways. For instance, when she realized that Elvire, her eldest daughter, had been converted to Catholicism by a very devout chamber maid, she never reproached her daughter, but promptly set about finding Elvire a husband with similar beliefs, because it made her very happy to do so. "I was the first person in Egypt," she observes, "who allowed her daughter to marry a Catholic [not an Egyptian, let us point out, but an Italian, to boot]. This was much frowned upon in our circle, and I was criticized; some family members even harboured resentment against me for a time. It was a civil marriage," she adds, the convivial side being never absent in her, "conducted at the Italian Consulate; the ceremony was quite lovely and intimate, and I wore a magnificent pearl-grey gown of faille.... After the ceremony Elvire, with her husband and their witnesses, went to the church, and I pretended not to notice anything. Very liberal in my ideas, I always felt the better for it"

The liberalness of ideas in France had struck a deep chord in her.

Then came the turn of her second daughter, Mathilde, who was destined to be Mother's mother. Mira Ismalun let her choose her own husband. Thus Mathilde Ismalun married a Turk by the name of Maurice Alfassa, a banker by profession. The marriage took place in Alexandria in 1874. "It was celebrated in grand style in the governmental palace," Mira Ismalun said in her charming way, "the Viceroy as well as all the Ministers attended. I had a magnificent gown and they found me more beautiful than my daughter."

Finally she settled down in France.

She stayed long enough in Egypt, however, to be present at the inauguration of the Suez Canal: "Monsieur de Lesseps came to fetch me with a cavalry escort." M. de Lesseps was an accomplished rider and his horsemanship had impressed even the Arabs. So, the two rode to the glittering reception given by Ismail Pasha in the recently built palace overlooking the new town on the canal bank, named Ismailia after the Khedive.

The canal was filled with the ships in which many crowned heads of Europe had sailed to the inauguration of the Suez Canal. But the pride of place went to the magnificent *l'Aigle* which had brought from France Empress Eugenie, wife of Napoleon III, along with Ferdinand de Lesseps. For it was indeed thanks to the royal backing that de Lesseps could complete his project.

But as they rode, M. de Lesseps' thoughts must have turned to his friend, Prince Said, who had died before completion of the canal. In his stead, his nephew, Ismail Pasha (who had taken the title of Khedive when he ascended the throne), was now declaring the Canal open.

Mira Ismalun knew how tenaciously Ferdinand de Lesseps had held on to his project through many ups and downs. Had he, perhaps, inherited Napoleon Bonaparte's dream? In 1798 Napoleon had discovered the ancient canal of the Pharaohs, lost in the mists of time. Now it was 1869. How long dreams take to mature! So Mira Ismalun must have lent a very sympathetic ear to the sixty-four-year-old Ferdinand de Lesseps as he spoke to her of the images that flitted through his white-haired head:

1854, November 15: A rainbow in the early morning sky, filling him with the hope of fulfilling his long-cherished dream. The ride on horseback to the camp of Prince Said, who succeeded his father, Mehemet Ali, as the Viceroy of Egypt. Obtaining his permission to dig the Suez Canal.

1859, April 25th: Taking hold of a spade and starting to dig near the bay of Pelusium. Passing on the spade to the team of his engineers and about a hundred men. Each in turn digging up a spadeful of earth. A quiet, unheralded beginning for an enormous project that took ten years to complete and an army of professionals working with heavy equipment.

1869, August 15th: The Red Sea joins the Mediterranean.

1869, November 17th: Today, the road to India is opened. A voyage of four months is now shortened to seventeen days.

Friends of such calibre had Mira Ismalun. Men capable of materializing their vision. And these men - and women - had a profound respect and admiration for her.

This little Arabian lady who took Paris by storm with her sky-blue pourpoint and her tarboosh tipped low, who read *The Origin of Species* and created havoc in the Grand Hotel, finally retired to Nice, where she spent the last years of her life, shuttling between the Mediterranean and the "calm shores of Lake Geneva." "After having frequented galas and theatres, swept through all the great capitals and spas, lived on intimate terms with celebrities - a grand existence in which I had no worry other than looking after my affairs and satisfying, if not my caprice, at least the legitimate desires of *la belle vie* - I had the wisdom to resign myself to a somewhat more modest and tranquil life...." Her husband "generally" accompanied her, she notes prosaically. "He worshipped me," which does not surprise us.

But the most unexpected in this impetuous and irresistible life, impatient of all frontiers, although emerging from the Valley of the Nile, is a sudden cry that broke from her lips at the end of this gala journey, as though all limits were unacceptable to her, including those of death: "Frankly speaking, at seventy-six I scarcely like old age, life is still beautiful to me... and I proclaim with Goethe, 'Beyond the tombs, forward !' "

From such seed came Mother.

Mother's Chronicles — Book One: MIRRA, by Sujata Nahar

The Mother in Kyoto, Japan, 1916

Those things about mummies...

In the physical form there is the 'spirit of the form,' and that spirit of the form persists for a time, even when outwardly the person is said to be dead. And as long as the spirit of the form persists, the body isn't destroyed. In ancient Egypt they had that knowledge; they knew that if they prepared the body in a certain way, the spirit of the form wouldn't go away and the body wouldn't be dissolved. In certain cases, they succeeded wonderfully. And if you go and violate the sleep of those beings who for thousands of years have remained like that, I can understand that they aren't too pleased, especially when their sleep is violated out of an unhealthy curiosity legitimized by scientific ideas. At the Guimet Museum in Paris, there are two mummies. Nothing remains in one; but in the other, the spirit of the form has remained very conscious, conscious to such a point that you can have a contact of consciousness with it. It's obvious that when a bunch of idiots come and stare at you with round eyes devoid of any understanding, saying, 'Oh, he is like this, he is like that,' it's not likely to please you. You know, in the first place they do something odious: those mummies are enclosed in a box with a special shape to fit the person, with everything needed to preserve them; so they open the box with more or less violence, they remove some wrapping here and there to see better.... And as ordinary people were never mummified, they were beings who had achieved a considerable inner power, or else members of the royal family, people of some initiation....

Playground Talk of March 10th, 1951

Mother's Agenda, Vol. 6, 27th February 1965

Those things about mummies, I knew them when I was nine or ten, they are memories from that time. I would find again some objects I had used in the past (that's how I was later able to rediscover the track). I had at least – at least – three incarnations in Egypt (three that have been found).

But my first contact took place when I was quite small, nine or ten, and it was with that mummy at the Guimet Museum: I was speaking about that experience.

Mother's Agenda, Vol. 6, 27th February 1965

But he is Amenhotep...

Mother's Agenda, Vol. 6, June 5th, 1965

*(Then Mother starts sorting old scattered notes
on all manner of slips of paper. She holds out to Satprem a first slip...)*

Mother: What is it?

Satprem: It's about young I.

Mother: Oh! I... I. is Amenhotep.

That was very amusing (I didn't tell his mother), but I saw him a year or two ago when he arrived from America with his parents. They came here to see me. I saw him, I wasn't thinking of anything, I was simply looking at him (meaning that I was taking him inside me). He wasn't quite like an ordinary child, he had rather princely manners. I noticed it, but nothing special apart from that. I saw him in the morning, then in the afternoon when I rested, I had a vision, that is to say, I relived a life in Egypt. It was ancient Egypt, I saw it from my costume, from the walls, from everything (I don't know if I have noted it there), anyway it wasn't modern. And I clearly was the Pharaoh's wife, or his sister (I don't remember now), and suddenly I said to myself, "This child is impossible! He keeps doing what he isn't supposed to do!" *(Mother laughs)* So I went out of my room, entered a great hall, and the little child was busy playing in a gutter! *(Laughing)* Which I found completely disgusting! So his tutor ran up to me immediately to tell me (I must have noted it):

Amenhotep III, Akhenaten, as a young prince
August Kestner Museum, Hannover, Germany

"Such is the will of Amenhotep."

That is how I knew his name.
What did I write?

"In ancient Egypt. A temple or palace of ancient Egypt. Light - and fresh-coloured paintings on the very high walls. Clear light. About the child, very bold, independent and playful, I hear the end of a sentence: 'Such is the will of Amenhotep.' The entire name is uttered very clearly, but when I got up (too abruptly), only the syllable 'tep' was retained by the memory of the waking consciousness. It was the tutor speaking to me about the child. I am the Pharaoh's wife or the high priestess of the temple, with full authority."

That was my first memory on waking up.
But he is Amenhotep.
What's written there?

It's a note on Amenhotep:

"Amenhotep III is the builder of Thebes and Luxor.... His palace, south of Thebes, was built with sun-dried bricks covered with painted stucco. His wife, Tiye, seems to have come from a higher family, but was showered with honours by him and their son. The son succeeded his father under the name of Amenhotep IV. He was a religious reformer who replaced the cult of Ammon with that of Aton (the Sun). He took the name of Akhenaten." [Encyclopedia Britannica]

Pharaoh Akhenaten,
Colossal statue from Karnak, Egyptian Museum, Cairo

That's the one.

He's a tough little fellow, dear me! They have a hard time with him.

I didn't tell his mother.

When they are here, everything is fine. But as soon as they go to Bombay, where the husband's family is, he falls ill, he becomes absolutely unbearable, he is impossible – here, he is controlled. And strangely enough, they put in his bedroom friezes of simplified animals (I saw some photos, they look very much like Egyptian paintings), and he is very happy there, very calm.

It's amusing.

And I wasn't thinking of anything at all; I was looking at that child (who is obviously a conscious and very self-assured being), I looked at him and it amused me; then I put it out of my mind. And later on, I had that vision and I knew it was he – I saw him. "Such is the will of Amenhotep."

Mother's Agenda, Vol. 6, June 5th, 1965

I was the high priestess...
so I know the child was Amenhotep

Mother's Agenda, May 10th, 1967

(Satprem reads Mother an old Playground talk of May 23, 1956, in which Mother suddenly asked various questions about the pronunciation of ancient Egyptian hieroglyphs.)

Satprem: Was there something special that triggered your questions?

Mother: At one time, I was very interested in knowing about it. I tried to recall the memory of the elements that lived at that time, but...

Satprem: Yes, you say, "I wondered how they retrieved the names of the pharaohs and gods." Then you ask, "Is the Egyptians' language contemporary with the most ancient Sanskrit, or still more ancient?... Or is there another human language older than the oldest Sanskrit?" You also ask, "Is this hieroglyphic Egyptian language akin to the Chaldean line or the Aryan line?"

Mother: Yes, all that is very interesting, but I can't get an answer. There's a complete lacuna.

Satprem: Had you heard sounds or what?

Mother: (After a silence) Listen, I'll give you an example. Some two years ago, I had a vision about U.'s son. She had brought him to me (he was almost one) and I had just seen him there [in the music room].

He struck me as someone I knew very well, but I didn't know who. Then, the same day in the afternoon, I had a vision. A vision of ancient Egypt, in which I was someone, the high priestess or I don't know who. (Because you don't say to yourself, "I am so and so"! The identification is total, there is no objectification, so I don't know.) I was inside a wonderful monument, immense, so high! But it was completely bare: there was nothing, except in one place where there were magnificent paintings. That's where I recognized the paintings of ancient Egypt. I was coming out of my apartments and entering a sort of large hall: there was a kind of gutter running on the ground all along the walls to collect water. And I saw the child playing in it, half-naked. I was very shocked, I said, "What! This is disgusting!" (But the feelings, ideas and so on were all translated into French in my consciousness.) The tutor came, I had him called. I scolded him. I heard sounds – well, I don't know what I said, I don't remember those sounds. I heard the sounds I uttered, I knew what they meant, but the translation was in French, and I didn't keep a memory of the sounds. I spoke to him, telling him, "What! You let this child play in that?" And he answered me (I woke up with his answer), saying (I didn't hear the first words, but to my thought it was), "Such is the will of Amenhotep." I heard "Amenhotep," I remembered it. So I knew the child was Amenhotep.[1]

Therefore, I know I spoke; I spoke in a certain language, but I don't remember. I remembered "Amenhotep" because I know the word Amenhotep in my active consciousness. But otherwise, the other sounds didn't stay. I don't have the memory of sounds.

And I know I was his mother; at that moment I found out who I was, because I know that Amenhotep is so and so's son (and also

----

1   Mother had recounted this vision before: *See Agenda VI of June 5, 1965, and Agenda IV of June 3, 1963*

Young Amenhotep III (Akhenaten)
August Kestner Museum, Hannover, Germany

I looked up in history books). Otherwise there's no connection: a blank.

I always admire those mediums (they generally are very simple people) who have the exact memory of the sound and can tell you, "This and that is what I said." That way we could have a phonetic notation. If I remembered the sounds I uttered we would have the notation, but I don't.

I remember these questions: I suddenly thought, "How interesting it would be to hear that language!" And then, a curiosity: "How did they rediscover the pronunciation? How?" Besides, all the names of ancient history we were taught when we were very small have been changed now. They said they rediscovered the sounds, or rather they claimed they did. But I don't know.

It's the same thing with ancient Babylon: I have extremely precise and perfectly objective memories, but when I speak I don't remember the sounds I utter, there is only the mental transcription.

I don't have the memory of sounds.

Mother: So how did they rediscover them? Do you know?

Satprem: By crosschecks. That's in fact what Pavitra explains to you. They found stones with inscriptions in Egyptian, Greek and Coptic: the same text in those three languages. So they pieced it together.

Mother: Now, with the phonograph and all that, the sounds will be remembered, but at that time they weren't noted.

Satprem: I wondered what gave rise to your questions.

Mother: That's what, the awareness that I don't have the memory of sounds. Some people have the memory of sounds, but I don't. So I'd be interested to know how it was. Otherwise I was always able (when I found something from the past doubtful or interesting or incomplete), I always found a way to recall it into the consciousness. But the sounds don't come. They come as a state of consciousness that's translated mentally, and it's translated mentally into words I know. So that's quite uninteresting.

Even now, even when I used to play music, the memory of sounds was vague and incomplete. I had the memory of the sounds I heard in the "origin of music" *(gesture above),* and when the material music reproduced something of those sounds, I would recognize them; but there isn't the precision, the accuracy that would enable me to reproduce exactly the sound with the voice or an instrument. It's not there, it's lacking. Whereas the memory of the eyes was... it was astounding. When I had seen a thing ONCE, that was enough, I would never forget it.

Several other times, in visions ("visions", I mean memories: relived memories), I spoke the language of that time, I spoke in it and heard myself speak, but the sound didn't stay. The MEANING of what I said stayed, but not the sound.

A pity.

(Mother goes into a meditation)

After the meditation,

Mother tells what she has seen:

It was the symbol of the road opening up, wide open, easy – not "easy": it's dangerous in itself, but quite easy, one travelled on it easily. It was as if riding in a car (but these are images), and it went with dizzying speed, like a power – a power nothing could stop. You were there.

Mother's Agenda, May 10th, 1967

Egypt was in an extremely occult age

Mother's Agenda, July 15th, 1967

Satprem: Before I came to India for the first time, I was twenty-two and knew nothing of spirituality or anything else, but I spent a month in Egypt, and for a month I lived in a state of extraordinary emotion, without knowing why.

Mother: Ah!

Satprem: I was in a state of constant emotion: everything held me spellbound. Egypt made an extraordinary impression on me.

Mother: Ah, but we lived together in Egypt. I've known you from the time of Egypt,[1] I know that. You are one of those to whom I said in Egypt, "I promise you that you will be part... that you will be on earth at the hour of realization." There are a few of them – not many *(Mother makes a gesture of being scattered across the world)*. But I know that!

I made that promise to a certain number of people – not all in the same age: at different stages.

Did you go to Thebes?

Satprem: Yes, I did.

Mother: Did you like it?

---

1   See also *Agenda* I, October 30, 1960

Satprem: Oh, it was... that's where I had the most emotion.

Mother: Exactly.   *(silence)*

I don't generally talk about these things because it fastens people to the past: they try to relive what they lived, so you understand, that spoils everything.

But it's a sort of sensation I have: it doesn't correspond to anything here *(gesture to the head)*, it's a sensation, the sensation of an atmosphere, or rather, of a kind of vibration which has already been felt, and so can easily be traced back to when and where.

Oh, there are amusing things.

Egypt was in an extremely occult age, at that time they really had occult knowledge. So that gives you a power over the invisible, you can act there consciously.

There was one thing (which I told you, I think): for a while (it didn't last long), for a few days, there was a sort of need to know how people spoke, the sounds that were used.[2] If I had insisted, it would probably have come: how I used to say things, how that consciousness used to express itself. That hasn't been preserved.

Our age will be far more durable in memory if things aren't destroyed – we'll just have to turn on a machine.

Satprem: Unfortunately, there won't be much worth preserving from our age!

Mother: Oh! That's a remarkable thing: in every age, and probably on the contrary, the farther you go into the past, there's a jumble, a clutter of quite uninteresting things – which disappear. They

---

2   See conversation of May 10, 1967 (Amenhotep)

disappear, they are destroyed. There only remains what had an interesting inner life. So the past seems to us much more interesting than the present, but from our age all the clutter will also disappear and be dissolved in the same way, and only the best will remain, except if they use mechanical means to preserve loads of recordings of heaps of stupidities. But otherwise...

I have, for instance, an impression (a strong impression) that in the Assyrian age they had a means, they had found a means to record and preserve sound. It must have been destroyed, it disappeared. But it's a very strong impression, linked to certain memories and [psychic] impressions like the ones I said: they aren't ideas, but [vibrations]. There was a capacity to make the invisible speak, you understand.

They had a machine. It must have been destroyed with the rest?

The oldest memory we have is the first Chinese attempts. It's in China that a machine to reproduce sound, to preserve and reproduce sound, was first found.

The Chinese were very inventive. *(silence)*

I had a very strong impression, which, so to speak, crystallized when I went to China[3] (I know nothing of China: a city or two, a port or two, that's nothing; but still you pick up a bit of the atmosphere): the origin of those people is lunar. There must have been beings living on the moon, and they (or a few of them, I don't know) took refuge on the earth when the moon was dying. And that was the origin of the Chinese race.
They are very peculiar. They don't at all have the same kind of vital being as all the other human beings, not at all.

---

3   In 1920, when Mother sailed back to Pondicherry from Japan, at the time
    when Mao Tse-tung was writing The Great Union of Popular Masses.

Theirs is a strange vital.

Satprem: What kind of vital?

Mother: Cold.

Cold: intellectual and cold. Cold. It's very insensitive. And the strange thing is that their sensitivity isn't the same at all, it's extremely dulled.

Mother's Agenda, July 15th, 1967

Akhet-Aten, Tell el-Amarna, Boundary Stele N

I saw their god with a sun above his head

Mother's Agenda, Vol.1, 30th October 1960

(After a meditation with Mother on the occasion of the disciple's birthday. At the outset of the conversation, Mother had given the disciple a small leather wallet with an Egyptian fresco depicted on it.)

Mother: Let me see the wallet *(Mother looks at it)* ... Ah, so that has nothing to do with it!

As soon as the meditation began, I started seeing quite familiar scenes from ancient Egypt. And you, you looked a little different, but quite similar all the same ... The first thing I saw was their god with a head like this *(gesture of a muzzle),* with a sun above his head. A dark animal head with ... I know it VERY WELL, but I don't remember exactly which animal it is. One is a hawk, but the other has a head like ... (Mother *makes the same gesture)*

Satprem: Like a jackal?

Mother: Yes, like a jackal, that's it. Yes, that's what it was. With a kind of lyre above its head, and then a sun.

And this god was very intimately related to you, as if you were melted together; you were like a sacrificial priest and at the same time he was entering into you.

And this lasted quite long (it's what I saw most clearly and what I best remember). But there were many, many things – old things that I know – and certainly a VERY INTIMATE relationship which we had in the days of Egypt, at Thebes.

It's the first time I saw this for you – it was very, very ...

'Was it by chance the wallet that brought this to mind?' I wondered right at first. I had the impression of having given you

The god Montu 'Lord of Thebes', with characteristic
solar disk and twin plumes, Karnak temple, Luxor

something Egyptian, but I could no longer remember what it was – I'm happy it wasn't that! ... I hesitated for barely a moment, then said to myself, 'Why?' And what came is that everything, even apparently accidental things, is organized by the same Consciousness for the same ends – it's obvious.

But I found this interesting, so I began looking, and I LIVED the scene, all kinds of scenes of initiation, worship, etc., for quite some time. When that lifted, a light much stronger than the last time *(during the last meditation)* came down, in a wonderful silence. (I might add that the first thing I did, at the beginning, was to try to establish a silence around you, to insulate you from other things so as to keep your mind quiet; it kept jumping a little, but once this light came down ...) And it came down with a very hieratic quality and ... (how can I put this?) Egyptian in character – very occult, very occult, very, very distinct, very specific, like this *(gesture indicating a block of silence descending).*

And then there came a long moment of absolutely motionless contemplation ... with something that now escapes me – it may come back.

Then suddenly I went into a little trance. And in it I saw you, but you were ... physically, you were on one plane, and then I saw another man on a different plane (I saw him quite concretely; he was rather tall, broad-shouldered – not so tall as broad, with a dark, European suit). And he took your hands and started shaking them enthusiastically! – but you were quite indifferent, just as you are now, dressed in Indian fashion and sitting cross-legged. He took both your hands and started shaking them! And then I distinctly heard the words: 'Congratulations, it's a great success!' – it had to do with your book.[241] And at the same time, I saw all sorts of people and things who were touched by your book – all kinds of people, obviously French, or Westerners in any case ... women,

men. There was even one woman (she must have been an actress or a singer or ... anyway, someone whose life was ... she was even dressed for the stage, with some kind of tights – a beautiful girl!) and she said to someone, 'Ah, it has even given me a taste for the spiritual life!' It was extremely interesting ... All kinds of things of this nature. And then once again I came out of this trance and ... In the end, I tried to do some certain thing for you and it turned out well. It turned out quite well.

But then, just before that, there was this powdering of golden light coming down. And as it descended, it was white with a touch of gold (but it was white) and it came down in a column, with such POWER! ... And then, just at the end, this powdering of gold came and settled into this white light which had remained there the whole time – oh, it was so ... abundant. A great power of realization. I had a hard time coming out of it! At the start, I had decided to come out of it at half past, so I came out, but still not completely ...

So there, my child. And you, what did you feel?

Satprem: When I meditate with you ... When I'm alone, there is never this power, this ... It's something else ... Sometimes it's strong but it always lacks this particular quality. There are powerful moments when I'm alone, but not like this.

Mother: Of course! I'm also with you there in your room when you meditate, but it does make a difference ...

L'Orpailleur, which had just been published. The man's description, as a matter of fact, bears a striking resemblance to the publisher.

The physical vibration is important. The circumstances relating to the work of transformation make the physical vibration important. I feel it, for as soon as I want to do something with someone on the physical plane (physical, mind you), it all comes

The unbroken seal on King Tutankhamun's tomb, 1922
(Tutankhaten, Akhenaten's son)

This seal was actually a seal to King Tut's fifth shrine. The king was buried in a series of four sarcophagi, which were in turn kept inside a series of five shrines. This unbroken seal stayed 3245 years untouched.

Harry Burton photographed the ornately decorated doors of the second shrine while closed, their simple copper handles secured together tightly by a rope tied through them. The knotted cord was accompanied by a delicate clay seal featuring Anubis, the ancient Egyptian's jackal god entrusted with the protection of the cemetery.

into the body. And the body is simply seized ... I see that absolutely physical vibrations are being used all the time. It's really so different.

All the work which is done at a distance *(gesture indicating action stemming from the mind)* – it acts, of course, but ...

You know, even now, all this *(Mother touches her body, her hands)* feels so vibrant and alive that it's difficult to sense its limits ... as if it extends beyond the body in all directions. It no longer has any limits.

But it's still not luminous in the dark. What is normally luminous in the dark is something else ... I had that when I was working with Theon (after returning to France, we had group meditations – though he didn't call it 'meditation', he called it 'repose', and we used to do this in a darkened room), and there was ... it was like phosphorescence, exactly the colour of phosphorescent light, like certain fish in the water at night. It would come out [of the body], spread forth, move about. But that is the vital, it originates in the vital. It is a force from above, but what manifests is vital. Whereas now it is absolutely, clearly the golden supramental light in ... an extraordinary pulsation, vibrant in intensity ... But probably it still lacks a ... what Theon used to call 'density,' an agent that enables it to be seen in the dark – and then it would be visibly gold, not phosphorescent.

But it is very, very concrete, very material.

I wonder if at night ... Sometimes it's so intense that I wonder if it doesn't radiate. But I can't see as my eyes are closed!

Again last night, for a large part of the night, it was ... the body has no more limits – it's only a great MASS of vibrations.

And the experience just now *(during meditation)* was somehow mixed with what I usually see at night (it was not a combination – or maybe it was a combination ...), for it had that same light ... It was a kind of powdering, even finer than tiny dots – a powdering like an atomic dust, but with an EXTREMELY intense vibration ...

but without any shifting of place. And yet it's in constant motion ... Something shifting about within something that vibrates on the same spot without moving (something does move, but it's subtler, like a current of tremendous power which passes through a milieu that doesn't move at all: rather, it vibrates on the same spot with an extreme intensity). But I don't exactly know how it is different from the present experience ... It becomes less golden at night, the gold is less visible, whereas the other colours – white, blue and a sort of pink – are much more visible.

Oh, now I remember! It was PINK during the second phase, just afterwards, after Egypt! Oh, it was like ... like at the end of a sunrise when it gets very clear and luminous. A magnificent colour.

And it kept coming down and down, in a flood ... that part was new. It's something I see very rarely. It was not there at all the last time we meditated together. And it came filled with such a joy!

Oh! ... It was absolutely ecstatic. It lasted quite a long time. And from there I went into this trance where I saw *(laughing)* that man congratulating you! I heard him say (his voice is what roused me from my trance, and then I saw him), 'Congratulations, it's a great success!' *(Mother laughs)*

It's good. We'll have these little meditations from time to time. For me, it's pleasant, for I have neither to restrict nor contain nor veil myself. It's nice.

And I see what's coming down; it's good.

And there is something very happy, very happy, which keeps repeating, 'It's good, it's good!'

Happy ... and rather satisfied because of that.

My impression is that in a while, maybe not in such a distant future, we'll be able to do something, a sort of ... it will no longer be personal. We should be able to establish something.

Mother's Agenda, Vol.1, 30th October 1960

Occultism was in ancient Egypt very developed...

Mother Agenda, Vol. 4, August 10th, 1963

Mother: ...But it's still going on. Now, there's a great battle against all the ideas, the habits, the sensations, the possibilities, everything, concerning death – "death" (*laughing*), not "death" in the sense of the consciousness departing (that, of course, people talk about, but... those things no longer exist), no: WHAT THE CELLS MUST FEEL.[1] And all the possibilities are presented to me... With that consciousness (the consciousness accumulated, compressed in all those cells), when the heart stops beating and it's understood that, according to human ignorance, you are "dead", how does the force that groups all those cells together abdicate its will to hold them all together?... Naturally, I was told right away (because the problem – all the problems – come from everywhere, and it's purposely that I am shown the problem and made to struggle with it; it's not just as an "idea"), I was told right away that that force, that consciousness which holds everything together in really superconscious cells (they don't have at all the ordinary type of consciousness; ordinarily, it's the inner, vital being [Mother touches the heart centre] that's conscious of oneness, that is, conscious of being a being), that this aggregate of cells is now an aggregate OF ITS OWN WILL, with an organized consciousness which is a sort of collective gathering of that cellular consciousness; well...

Obviously this is an exceptional condition, but even in the past, in those beings who were very developed outwardly, there

---

1   After "death" or at the time of "death"

was a beginning of willed, conscious cellular gathering, and that's
certainly why in ancient Egypt, where occultism was very developed.
exceptional beings such as the pharaohs, the high priests, etc., were
mummified, so as to preserve the form as long as possible. Even
here in India, generally they were petrified (in the Himalayas there
were petrifactive springs). There was a reason.[2]

And I saw for Sri Aurobindo (although he hadn't yet started this
systematic transformation; but still, he was constantly pulling the
supramental force down into his body), even in his case, it took
five days to show the first slight sign of decomposition.

I would have kept his body longer, but the government always
meddles in other people's business, naturally, and they pestered
me awfully, saying it was forbidden to keep a body so long and
that we should... So when the body began to (what's the word?)
shrink – it was shrinking and contracting, that is, dehydrating –
then we had to do it. He had had enough time to come out, since
almost everything came into my body – almost everything that was
material came into my body....

Mother's Agenda, Vol. 4, August 10th, 1963

---

2   Many years earlier, Mother had told Satprem a vision she had had of one of
    her bodies petrified in a Himalayan cave, near a route of pilgrimage.

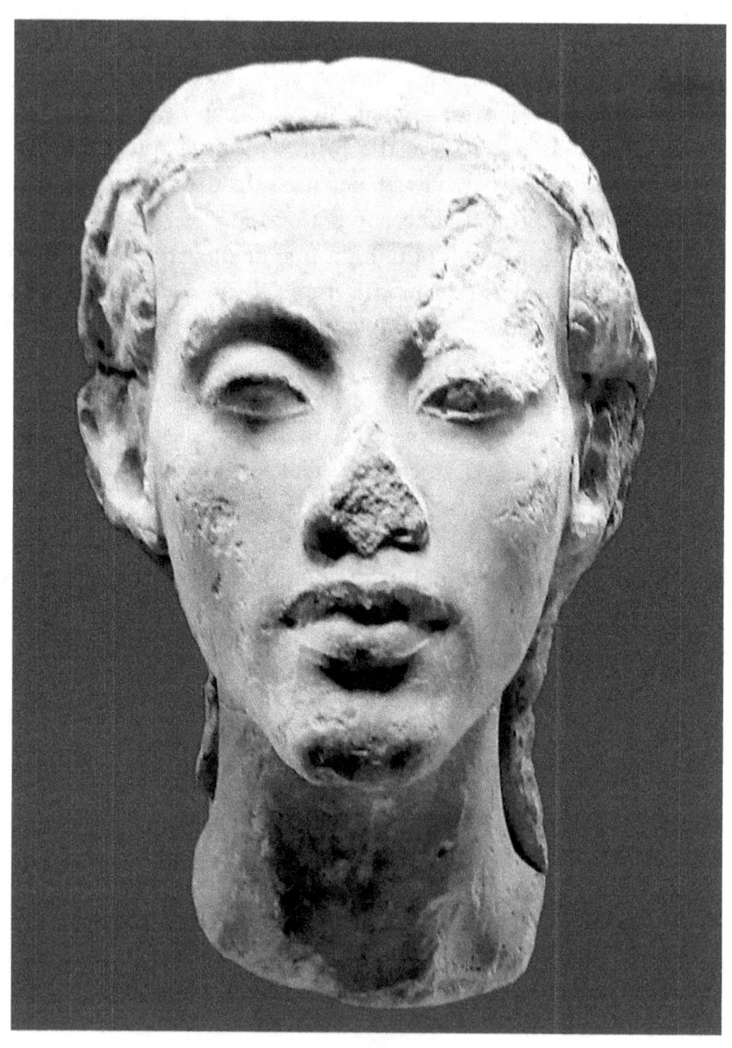

Prince Akhenaten
found in the Amarna workshop of the Royal Artisan Thutmose
Neues Museum, Berlin

The gods of India are very much alive

(Later, Mother again speaks of her vision of the tall white being armed with a kind of halberd.)

Mother: What was standing there was a manifestation of one of my states of being, a part of my vital being, or rather one of my innumerable vital beings – because I have quite a few! And this one is particularly interested in things on earth.

Satprem: A projection of yours – an emanation?

Mother: You know, mon petit, I said one day that in the history of earth, wherever there was a possibility for the Consciousness to manifest, I was there[1]; this is a fact. It's like the story of *Savitri:* always there, always there, always there, in this one, that one – at certain times there were four emanations simultaneously!

At the time of the Italian and French Renaissance. And again at the time of Christ, then too.... Oh, you know, I have remembered so many, many things! It would take volumes to tell it all.

And then, more often than not (not always, but more often than not), what took part in this or that life was a particular yogic formation of the vital being – in other words something immortal.[2]

---

1   Since the beginning of the earth, wherever and whenever there was the possibility of manifesting a ray of the Consciousness, I was there." March 14, 1952.

2   Each of these formations had an independent, immortal existence.

And when I came this time, as soon as I took up the yoga, they came back again from all sides, they were waiting.

Some were simply waiting, others were working (they led their own independent lives) and they all gathered together again. That's how I got those memories. One after the other, those vital beings came – a deluge! I had barely enough time to assimilate one, to see, situate and integrate it, and another would come. They are quite independent, of course, they do their own work, but they are very centralized all the same. And there are all kinds – all kinds, anything you can imagine! Some of them have even been in men: they are not exclusively feminine.

At first, I used to think they were fantasies.

Before I met Sri Aurobindo they would come and come and come to me, night after night and sometimes during the day – a mass of things! Afterwards I told Sri Aurobindo about it, and he explained to me that it was quite natural. And indeed, it is quite natural: with the present incarnation of the Mahashakti (as he described it in *Savitri*), whatever is more or less bound up with Her wants to take part, that's quite natural. And it's particularly true for the vital: there has always been a preoccupation with organizing, centralizing, developing and unifying the vital forces, and controlling them. So there's a considerable number of vital beings, each with its own particular ability, who have played their role in history and now return. But this one [the tall white Being] is not of human origin; it was not formed in a human life: it is a being that had already incarnated, and is one of those who presided over the formation of this present being [Mother]. But, as I said, I saw it: it was sexless, neither male nor female, and as intrepid as the vital can be, with a calm but absolute power.... Ah, I found a very good description of it in one of Sri Aurobindo's plays, when he speaks of the goddess Athena (I think it's in *Perseus,* but I am not sure); she has that kind of... it's an almighty calm, and with such authority! Yes, it's in *Perseus* – when she appears to the Sea-God and forces him to retreat to his own domain. There's a description there that fits this Being quite well.[3]

Besides, all the Greek gods are various aspects of a single thing: you see it this way, that way, that way, this way *(turning her hand, Mother seems to show several facets of a single prism)....* But it's simply one and the same thing.[4]

Sri Aurobindo's description fits this Being exactly. And a few days ago, this same Being came, without my calling it or thinking about it or wishing it to come. And it seemed to be saying it was time for it to intervene.

So I let it!

During the whole time Sri Aurobindo was here, the four entities he speaks of, the four Aspects of the Mother,[114] were always present. And I was constantly obliged to tell one or the other of them, "Now keep calm, now, now, calm down" – they were always inclined to intervene!

Did I ever tell you? Last time I went down for the pujas (was it last year or the year before? I remember nothing any more, you know: it all gets swept away, brrt!).... Yes, it was the year before last,

---

3   A whiteness and a strength is in the skies...
Virgin formidable
In beauty, disturber of the ancient world! ...
How art thou white and beautiful and calm,
Yet clothed in tumult! Heaven above thee shakes
Wounded with lightnings, goddess, and the sea
Flees from thy dreadful tranquil feet.

4   "They are different aspects of one self-existent thing," Mother clarified. "These beings have merely taken on different aspects depending on the country or the culture."

in '60, after that anniversary.115 (Durga used to come every year, two or three days before the Durga puja.) I was walking as usual and she came; that was when she made her surrender to the Supreme.... Those divinities don't have the sense of surrender. Divinities such as Durga and the Greek gods (although the Greek gods are a bit dated now; but the gods of India are still very much alive!). Well, they are embodiments – what you might almost call localizations – of something eternal, but they lack the sense of surrender to the Supreme. And while I was walking, Durga was there – really, it was beautiful! Durga, with that awesome power of hers, forever bringing the adverse forces to heel – and she surrendered to the Supreme, to the point of no longer even recognizing the adverse forces: ALL is the Supreme. It was like a widening of her consciousness.

Some interesting things have been happening in that world [since the supramental descent].... How can I explain? Those beings have an independence, an absolute freedom of movement (although at the same time, they are all a single Being), but they had the true sense of perfect Unity only with the supreme Consciousness. And now with this present intervention [Mother's], with this incarnation and the establishment of the Consciousness here, like this *(Mother makes a fist in a gesture of immutable solidity),* in such an absolute way (I mean there are no fluctuations)... HERE, on earth, in the terrestrial atmosphere, this incarnation has a radiating action throughout all those worlds, all those universes, all those Entities. And it results in small events,[5] incidents scaled to the size of the earth – which in themselves are quite interesting.

Mother's Agenda 3, June 27th, 1962

---

5   Like the one Mother just mentioned: Durga's surrender.

A gold mask protected the head and breast of Tutankhamun's mummy.
A collar of floral wreaths adorned the young deceased King,
Akhenaten's son. Photo from 1923

I have been in contact with all those gods

Mother's Agenda 3, June 30th, 1962

(A little later, Mother refers to a passage from the preceding conversation in which she said that her present incarnation on earth didn't have a merely terrestrial effect but an effect on all the other worlds as well – and particularly on the gods.)

Mother: None of those beings, those gods and deities of various pantheons, have the same rapport with the Supreme that man has; for man has a psychic being, in other words, the Supreme's presence within him.

These gods are emanations – independent emanations – created for a special purpose and a particular action which they fulfill SPONTANEOUSLY; they do it not with a sense of constant surrender to the Divine but simply because that's what they are, and why they are, and all they know is what they are.

They don't have the conscious link with the Supreme that man has – man carries the Supreme within himself.

That makes a considerable difference.

But with this present incarnation of the Mahashakti.... She is the Supreme's first manifestation, creation's first stride, and it was She who first gave form to all those beings. Now, since her incarnation in the physical world, and through the position She has taken here in relation to the Supreme by incarnating in a human body, all the other worlds have been influenced, and influenced in an extremely interesting way.[1] I have been in contact with all those gods, all those great beings, and for the most part their attitude has changed. And even with those who didn't want to change, it has nonetheless influenced their way of being.

Human experience, with this direct incarnation of the Supreme,[2] is ultimately a UNIQUE experience, which has given a new orientation to universal history. Sri Aurobindo speaks of this – he speaks of the difference between the Vedic era, the Vedic way of relating to the Supreme, and the advent of Vedanta (I think it's Vedanta): devotion, adoration, *bhakti,* the God within.[3] Well, this

---

1 Some days later, Satprem again brought up the above passage, asking whether the Mother hadn't been active on earth since the beginning of time and not merely "with this present incarnation of the Mahashakti." The reply: "It was always through EMANATIONS, while now it's as Sri Aurobindo writes in *Savitri* – the Supreme tells Savitri that a day will come when the earth is ready and 'The Mighty Mother shall take birth'.... But Savitri was already on earth – she was an emanation. *So they were all emanations?* They were all emanations, right from the beginning. So we have to say: 'With the PRESENT incarnation.'"

2. e., with the psychic being or soul IN MAN, the direct incarnation of the Supreme in man: "This has come with humankind."

3. Satprem subsequently asked Mother:
You almost seem to be saying that during the Vedic era there was no divine presence in man!
No, there wasn't! They discovered it.
"Humanity has undergone a spiritual evolution.
Vedism is in contact with the gods and, THROUGH THE GODS, with the Supreme; but it is not in direct contact with the Supreme – there is no inner, psychic contact".
That's what Sri Aurobindo says (I myself know nothing about it!). But with the Vedanta and the devotees of Krishna, it is the god within: they had a direct contact with the god within (as in the Gita).

aspect of rapport with the Supreme could exist ONLY WITH MAN, because man is a special being in universal history – the divine Presence is in him. And several of those great gods have taken human bodies JUST TO HAVE THAT.[4] But not many of them – they were so fully aware of their own perfect independence and their almightiness that they didn't NEED anything (unlike man, you see, struggling to escape his slavery): they were absolutely free.

And that's why.... How many times Durga came! She would always come, and I had my eye on her(!), because in her presence I could clearly sense that there wasn't that rapport with the Supreme (she just didn't need it, she didn't need anything). And it wasn't that something acted on her consciously, deliberately, to obtain that result: it has been a contagion. I remember how she used to come, and my aspiration would be so intense, my inner attitude so concentrated... and one day there was such a sense of power, of immensity, of ineffable bliss in the contact with the Supreme (it was a day when Durga was there), and she seemed to be taken and absorbed in it. And through that bliss she made her surrender.

Most interesting.

Not at all the result of will or anything: she was simply engulfed.

In those movements of consciousness, in this state of

---

4. Shortly afterwards, Satprem asked:
When a god takes a human body it must be terrible for him. Or does his divinity become quite veiled to him?
Yes, quite veiled.
They are powerful beings, they give a sense of power, but it is quite veiled.
But Krishna had a human body, Shiva had a human body.
But supposing one of those gods were to incarnate in the present world ... well, it wouldn't be much fun – he would suffocate.
Fun?... No, you see, they extend sufficiently beyond the limits of their bodies so as not to be suffocated.

consciousness, I am comfortable *(Mother heaves a sigh).* But it has taken me a lot of discipline to concentrate here [in the body]: there was always something, from my very childhood, that felt hemmed in, squeezed, really... Oh! And with a sense of something so powerful that if it ever went into action *(gesture of unleashing),* it would smash everything.

Now it has been tamed.

So, is that enough for you?

Satprem: No, no!   *(Mother laughs)*

Mother's Agenda 3, June 30th, 1962

The Mother's Egyptian Crown

On 1-5-1957 the Mother sent me (*to Huta*) her embroidered Egyptian crown which had two wings, one on either side of a bird. She asked me to paint only a profile of the bird. I finished the painting on 4-5-57 and showed it to her. The Mother liked the painting very much and asked me:

Child, can you draw a face with the crown which you have painted?

I replied:

Yes, Mother; I will try.

Afterwards she made several sketches of a face with the crown in order to show me how it could be done. Then suddenly she looked at me and said:

Ah! but you know that I have features like an Egyptian.

I caught a hint! I found one of the Mother's photographs in the Japanese dress—kimono—and sketched her face and showed it to the Mother in her room at the Playground. She saw my sketch. Amusement quivered in her voice as she asked me:

Child, from which photograph have you done this sketch?

I showed her the photograph. She exclaimed:

Here is the portrait of the Supreme Mother.

Well, eyes, lips and nose are not correct. Do you mind if I alter the drawing?

I replied:

Not at all, Mother.

Then she opened a painted glass-box sent to the Mother by my younger sister, Usha from East Africa. She took out her hand-mirror and gazed at her reflection in it. It was a thrilling sight to watch the Mother do her own portrait with so much concentration and serenity. Time and again her lips were touched by a sweet smile.

After completing it, and handing the sheet of paper to me, she said joyously:

Ah! Voilà! the Supreme Mother herself came and showed her face. In this picture dwells my soul, and I give it to you. Indeed, you are a very lucky girl!

I was so much moved that I could not utter a word. She took my face between her hands and looked at me intently. There was a warm deep glow in her eyes with an exceptional charm I had never seen before. Then she drew me closer and pressed my head against her heart. I felt immense relief and peace.

Here is the portrait of the Supreme Mother.

Huta D. Hindocha, The Spirit of Auroville, pp. 19-20
Havyavāhana Trust, 2002

Huta wrote also:

I feel that the Matrimandir in Auroville is the final temple the Mother wanted on earth to fulfill her vision of the Supreme Truth and Love in her New World.

In 1952, on our way to England, one of my brothers and his wife and I stayed in Cairo for two or three days. It was the night of the 23rd July, when King Farouk went into exile after General Mohammed Naguib seized power in Egypt. The very night our plane touched down in Cairo the King was leaving. At the airport everyone seemed to be excited and talking about the King.

During our stay in Cairo, I found everything familiar. I did not know why, I was entranced by the gigantic Pyramids and the famous Sphinx. While looking at the photographs which were taken there by us, I am reminded of one of the Mother's writings:

O serene and immobile Consciousness, Thou watchest on the boundaries of the world like a sphinx of eternity. And yet to some Thou givest out Thy secret. They can become Thy sovereign Will which chooses without preference and executes without desire.

This is a very beautiful passage written by the Mother:

This immobile Consciousness is the "Mother of Dreams", you may say that it is the creative consciousness, the origin of the Universe, the Universal Mother, the Creative Power - the sphinx of eternity who keeps vigil on the confines of the world like an enigma to be solved. This enigma is the problem of our life, the very raison d'etre of the Universe. The Problem of our life is to realise the Divine or rather to become once again aware of the Divine who is the Universe, the Origin, cause and goal of life. Those who find the secret of the Sphinx of Eternity become that active and Creative Power.

Huta D. Hindocha, The Spirit of Auroville, pp. 105-106
Havyavāhana Trust, 2002

You can discover the whole history of creation...

Satprem: One can remember things which happened thousands of years ago!

Mother: Yes, if you go to a certain place, if you succeed in entering into contact with the place which existed thousands of years ago. And, moreover (I believe I have written this somewhere), there is the record of the earth's consciousness, and if you know how to go to that place, you can not only remember your own life but everything that happened upon earth. It is recorded there, and it is a phenomenon of consciousness.

Satprem: But how does one remember, Sweet Mother, for when one changes the body, the mind...

Mother: I have just told you how, my child, you did not listen to what I said. I said that if it is a mental remembrance it will be effaced; even in your present life you cannot recall incidents which took place twenty or thirty or forty years ago. But a state of consciousness is not a mental state. It has nothing to do with the mind. Indeed, most minds are dissolved with the body, except when there is a very well-made special formation, very "cohesive", very well organised, which can last. But that is fairly rare. These are only exceptional cases. But consciousness is something quite different. Consciousness is an eternal state. The state of consciousness is an eternal state. Creation is born through consciousness and if consciousness were withdrawn, there would be no creation any longer. And if you enter into contact with consciousness, you can discover the whole history of creation, for creation comes from consciousness. Consciousness is eternal.

CWS, Questions and Answers, Vol. 6, 10th February 1954

The Mother, Mira Alfassa, Pondicherry

The true remembrance of past births...

How many of us remember former lives?

In all, in some part of our consciousness, there is a remembrance. But this is a dangerous subject, because the human mind is too fond of romance. As soon as it comes to know something of this truth of rebirth, it wants to build up beautiful stories around it. Many people would tell you wonderful tales of how the world was built and how it will proceed in the future, how and where you were born in the past and what you will be hereafter, the lives you have lived and the lives you will still live. All this has nothing to do with spiritual life.

The true remembrance of past births may indeed be part of an integral knowledge; but it cannot be got by that way of imaginative fancies. If it is on one side an objective knowledge, on the other it depends largely on personal and subjective experience, and here there is much chance of invention, distortion or false building. To reach the truth of these things, your experiencing consciousness must be pure and limpid, free from any mental interference or any vital interference, liberated from your personal notions and feelings and from your mind's habit of interpreting or explaining it in its own way.

An experience of past lives may be true, but between what you have seen and your mind's explanation or construction about it there is bound to be always a great gulf. It is only when you can rise above human feelings and get back from your mind, that you can reach the truth.

CWS, Questions and Answers, 5th May 1929

Queen Hatshepsut, Metropolitan Museum, New York

The Light of the Supreme

Sri Aurobindo was once asked by one of his young disciples Nagin Doshi what he and the Mother had been doing in their former births. "Carrying on the evolution" was the answer that he received from his Guru. When asked to elaborate, Sri Aurobindo wrote back: "That would mean writing the whole of human history. I can only say that as there are special descents to carry on the evolution to a farther stage, so also something of the Divine is always there to help through each stage itself in one direction or another."

✳

Both Sri Aurobindo and the Mother took birth to foster the progress of evolution of mankind and in each birth they played a very significant role. Each birth was unique in its own way: sometimes they came as rulers, sometimes as warriors and sometimes as artists or philosophers. As artists, their artistic creations are still admired; as philosophers, their works are still read even after the passing of several centuries. As rulers and warriors, their contribution to the society is still remembered. But what remain unknown are the former incarnations of Sri Aurobindo and the Mother. Sri Aurobindo has always been very silent about his past births but compared to him the Mother was more expressive and she spoke about her former births only in passing. As a matter of fact she, along with Nolini Kanta Gupta, has been the primary source of information about hers and Sri Aurobindo's previous incarnations.

As discussed earlier the Mother, unlike Sri Aurobindo, has spoken about her past incarnations, some of which she has described in some detail. According to her, her very first birth in a human form was in the earthly paradise about which she has spoken in detail in her 'On Thoughts and Aphorisms'. She has spoken of having 'at least' three births in Egypt; among them she has spoken at length about two, and the source of the information regarding the third birth is K.D. Sethna. The incarnations were Queen Hatshepsut (1504 − 1483 BCE), Queen Tiye (1397 − 60 BCE) and Queen Cleopatra (January 69 − 12 August 30 BCE), the Hellenistic ruler of Egypt who shared power first with her father Ptolemy XII and later with her brothers/husbands Ptolemy XIII and Ptolemy XIV. We have an interesting passage in 'Glimpses of the Mother's Life' which is as follows.

✳

"Standing in front of a portrait of Queen Hatshepsut, the Mother told the following story when she came to the Ashram's University Centre Library to open an exhibition on ancient Egypt in August 1954. When she was a girl of about eight or ten, she and her brother were taken one day by her teacher to the famous Museum of the Louvre in Paris. On the ground floor are galleries of Egyptian antiquities. As they were slowly passing through the collections, the Mother was suddenly attracted by a beautiful toilet case inlaid with gold and lapis lazuli, which was exposed in one of the museum cases. An attendant noticed her great interest and explained to her that the toilet case had belonged to the Egyptian Queen Hatshepsut. He also showed her a fine portrait of the Queen as a young girl and smilingly remarked that she had a striking resemblance to that ancient Queen. The toilet case and particularly the comb appeared to be strangely familiar to the Mother."

Pournaprema, the Mother's granddaughter, also writes in her book on the Mother: 'During this journey [from Paris to Pondicherry in March 1914] which led her towards Sri Aurobindo, she had to pass through the Suez Canal, and the Japanese ship in which she travelled stopped at Cairo in Egypt. She got off the ship there and went to visit the Cairo museum. Here in a glass showcase were exhibited the toilet-set of a great queen of Egypt: a comb, hair pins, perfume bottles and a jar for cosmetic cream. And looking at them, Douce Mére said, "How badly they've all been arranged. Not at all the way they were when I used to arrange them myself. The hairpins should have been there, the comb here and the bottles kept in this order…" She was used to seeing her things kept in a certain way, so she felt extremely annoyed now to find them placed differently…

✳

'Not until she was in the carriage going back to the port after leaving the museum did the real significance of what happened strike her - she had been this great Egyptian queen.' 'This great Egyptian queen' was none other than Queen Hatshepsut.

✳

About her birth as Queen Tiye (whose son Amenhotep IV [1376 – 47 BCE] would become the future Akhenaten), the Mother has said in May 1956: 'About two years ago I had a vision in connection with Z's son. She had brought him to me - he was not quite one year old - so I had just seen him in the room where I receive people. He gave me the impression of someone very well known to me, but I didn't know who or what. Then, in the afternoon of the same day, I had a vision. It was a vision of ancient Egypt, and I was somebody there: I was the High Priestess, or whomever. I didn't know whom, for one doesn't tell oneself "I am so-and-so." The identification is complete, there is no objectivation, so I don't know.

✹

I was in an admirable building, immense! so high! – but quite bare. There was nothing, except a place with magnificent paintings, which I recognized as the paintings of ancient Egypt. I was coming out of my apartments and entering a kind of large hall. There was a sort of gutter all along the walls, for collecting the water. And then I saw the child, half-naked, playing in it. I was quite shocked. I said: "What is this! This is disgusting!" (The feelings, ideas and all that were translated into French in my consciousness.) Then the tutor came – I had him called. I gave him a scolding. I heard the sounds. I don't know what I said, I don't remember the sounds any more. I heard the sounds I was pronouncing, I knew their meaning, but the translation was in French and the sounds I didn't remember. I spoke to [the tutor]. I told him: "How can you let the child play in there?" He answered - and I woke up with his reply - saying… I did not hear the first words, but in my thought it was [translated as]: "Amenhotep likes it." "Amenhotep" I heard and I remembered. Then I knew the little one had been Amenhotep.

✹

So I know that I spoke. I spoke in that language, but I don't remember it now. I remembered "Amenhotep" because I have kept that in my active consciousness: "Amenhotep." But the rest, the other sounds did not remain. I have no memory for sounds. And

The Mother in Tokyo, 1916

I know I was his mother. Then I knew who I was, for I know that Amenhotep was the son of so-and-so. Besides, I looked it up in history.'

✳

Georges Van Vrekhem has included a personal communication to him from Tanmaya, a French teacher who taught at the Ashram School for many years. In his biography of the Mother where the latter remembers: "In reply to a question (concerning Akhenaten) I had put to her, Mother let it clearly be understood that she had been Queen Tiye, the mother of Akhenaten... She specified that Akhenaten's revolution was intended to reveal to the people of that time the unity of the Divine and his manifestation. This attempt, the Mother added, was premature, for the human mind was not yet ready for it. It had, however, to be undertaken in order to assure the continuity of its existence in the mental plane."

✳

And Georges Van Vrekhem himself observes: "Tiye was a 'Vibhuti' of the Universal Mother, a fact which endowed her with the awareness of her eternal soul within, and thus of the Divine. She had probably become an initiate of the mysteries of Heliopolis, keeper of the secrets of the Sun. Here it is worth mentioning that Sri Aurobindo said that the Sun is the symbol of the Supramental, which is the Divine upholding all creation. (This upholding and blessing is graphically represented in Akhenaten's iconography of the Sun disk.) Having become a high occult initiate, Tiye may have had the vision or inspiration – or a series of visions or inspirations – of the supramental Truth. The word 'supramental

262

Truth' is nothing but a verbal abstraction for a divine Reality which surpasses everything an ordinary human being can feel, imagine and experience. It is the One Reality present in all that exists and of which the gods are the cosmic powers."

✸

According to K.D. Also, the sun stands universally for the whether the Mother herself has said anything about this particular incarnation of hers.

The Light of the Supreme, Journals
The former Incarnations of Sri Aurobindo and the Mother
20th April 2009, by Anurag Banerjee

I suddenly realized how far we were from really knowing Akhenaten

It is not just your Pharaoh's soul which illumines each of these words, but the soul of a great being who exceeds us all. When I discovered this invocation the other day, a short while after he himself had put it in my hands, I suddenly realized how far we were from really knowing Akhenaten.

The beauty of these sentences he has engraved with his own hand puts me in contact with his true nature. His soul, you see, is winged, more than any other. At the bottom of his heart, he doesn't care for the power his crown gives him, he uses it only to give to Love, to the True and to the Beautiful, a chance to find at last really a place in this world... and he is the only one to carry this to such a supreme degree.

I'm afraid he will remain for ever an enigma, not only for the times to come, but also for us. I'm afraid also that we only see in him the king brandishing a crazy ideal, when actually there is much more. I seem to discern now in his stature... I don't know how to say... the man drunk with the Sun, the man we all ought to be or to become. And this, such a man, is so much more than a Pharaoh! Of course I have always known all this, but never did I realize it as fully as today.

Daniel Meurois-Givaudan
Daniel Meurois-Givaudan, La Demeure de Rayonnat
Editions Le Perséa, 1998

House altar. King Akhenaten, Queen Nefertiti and three daughters.
New Museum, Berlin

Akhenaten and the Symbol of the Sun

Most often, Akhenaten was depicted as
being below the sun whose rays ended
with hands blessing him. For him,
the sun is Aten, the unique Divine living in all
and everywhere, symbol of the Truth, Love,
Peace and Beauty.

✸

"It is therefore under the images of
the sun and its rays, ...that the Aryan seers
[or Vedic Rishis] represent the progressive
illumination of the human soul?

✸

"Also, the sun stands universally for
the supramental Light, the divine Gnosis?"

✸

"The sun is the symbol
of the concentrated light of Truth?"

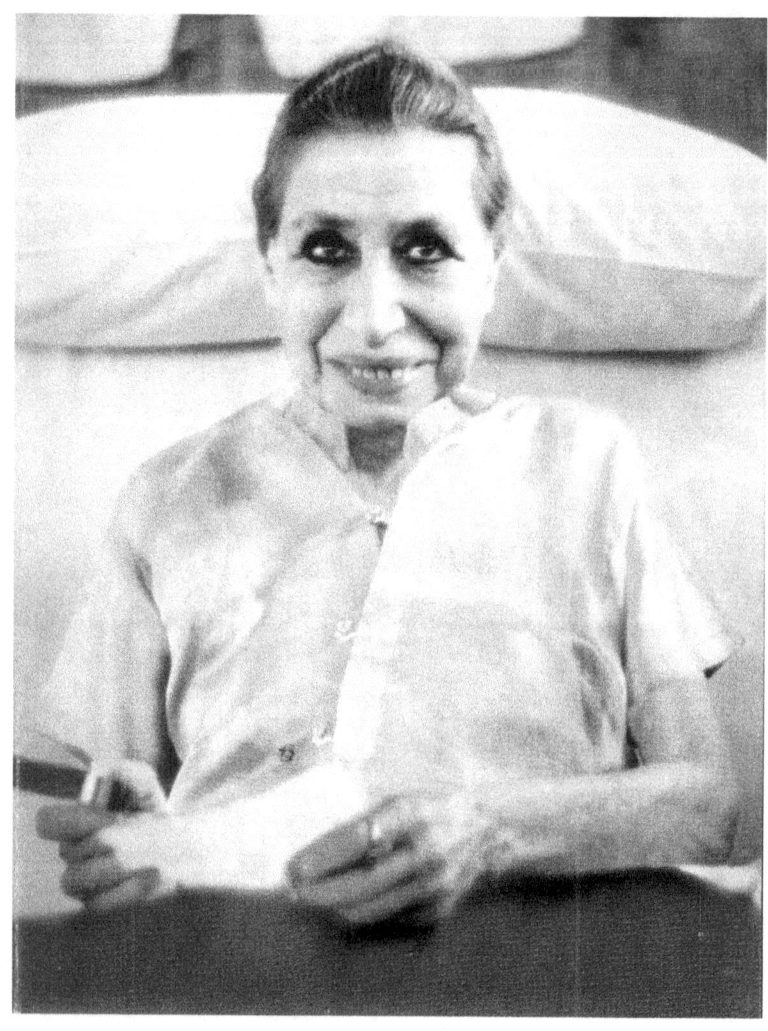

The Mother - Mirra Alfassa

Since the beginning of the earth,
wherever and whenever there was the
possibility of manifesting a ray of the
Consciousness, I was there.

The Mother

Mother's Agenda, Vol. I, 14th March 1952

At the Rising of the Sun...

At the rising of the sun I sang the praise of this world in which it is possible not only to desire Thee but to know Thee and even to become Thee. And I was astonished that there should be some who so ardently aspire to leave this universe and enter another world of perfection.

Thou hast placed such contentment in my heart that it has become impossible for me not to feel satisfied in all circumstances, inner or outer. And yet something in my being always aspires for more beauty, for more light, for more knowledge, for more love – in a word, for a more conscious, a more constant relation with Thee…. But this too depends upon Thy will, and when it is Thy will, Thou shalt grant me the entire transfiguration.

The Mother, Prayers and Meditations, July 25th, 1914

Cling to Truth.

✳

O Splendour of eternal Truth
I call Thee.
I salute Thee, O Sun of the morrow.

July 1971

✳

Supreme Lord, Eternal Truth
Let us obey Thee alone
and live according to
Truth.

June 1971

✳

When you are conscious of the whole world
at the same time, then you can become
conscious of the Divine.

January 1st 1973

Dreaming the Dream

A Dream: There should be somewhere upon earth a place that no nation could claim as its sole property, a place where all human beings of good will, sincere in their aspiration, could live freely as citizens of the world, obeying one single authority, that of the supreme Truth; a place of peace, concord, harmony, where all the fighting instincts of man would be used exclusively to conquer the causes of his suffering and misery, to surmount his weakness and ignorance, to triumph over his limitations and incapacities; a place where the needs of the spirit and the care for progress would get precedence over the satisfaction of desires and passions, the seeking for pleasures and material enjoyment.

In this place, children would be able to grow and develop integrally without losing contact with their soul. Education would be given, not with a view to passing examinations and getting certificates and posts, but for enriching the existing faculties and bringing forth new ones. In this place, titles and positions would be supplanted by opportunities to serve and organise.

The needs of the body will be provided for equally in the case of each and every one. In the general organisation intellectual, moral and spiritual superiority will find expression not in the enhancement of the pleasures and powers of life but in the increase of duties and responsibilities. Artistic beauty in all forms, painting, sculpture, music, literature, will be available equally to all, the opportunity to share in the joys they bring being limited solely by each one's capacities and not by one's social or financial position.

For in this ideal place money would be no more the sovereign lord. Individual merit will have a greater importance than the value due to material wealth and social position. Work would not be there as the means of gaining one's livelihood, it would be the means whereby to express oneself, develop one's capacities and possibilities, while doing at the same time service to the whole group, which on its side would provide for each one's subsistence and for the field of his work.

In brief, it would be a place where relations between human beings, usually based almost exclusively upon competition and strife, would be replaced by relations of emulation for doing better, for collaboration, relations of real brotherhood.

The earth is certainly not ready to realise such an ideal, for mankind does not yet possess the necessary knowledge to understand and accept it or the indispensable conscious force to execute it. That is why I call it a dream.

- *The Mother*

New Horizon *(Akhet-Aten)*

In the year 1956 Mother makes a second attempt to develop a new township - this time by the East side bank of Ossudu (Usteri) Lake. As was the case in Her first attempt (in the then Hyderabad State), She asks Antonin Raymond to be its architect.

Excerpt of a conversation with Satprem on 20.8.60. While filing various old papers, notes, etc., Mother happens upon the plan for a film studio at the lake some five miles from Pondicherry.

It's at the lake. The property belonged to the mission and at that time its manager was a very good friend of ours, even though he was a missionary. He said that they wanted to sell and that he would arrange for us to have it. Everything was arranged, and I was to receive the money to buy it (they asked for more than fifty or sixty thousand [rupees]). But then the money didn't come and our missionary friend left. He's no longer there; he's been replaced by someone else.

[Mother looks at a piece of paper]
"Calling Antonin Raymond" the architect for the construction. Then there was also "making ready temporary quarters for [an American film maker] Dr. Alexander Markey". But then Markey left; he died [in 1958]. That's what happens - things change. It's not that the project stops, but it's forced to take other paths.

Satprem: But this film project has been completely abandoned now, hasn't it?

No, no. You see, it wasn't a studio - it was a school, a school of photography, television and film. It's not at all buried. But Louis has enlarged the program. [Mother indicates the plan.] This is only a small part of his extensive total program. He is planning to have a school of agriculture, a modern dairy with grazing land - there's a lot of agriculture, really a lot - fruit orchards, large rice fields, many things. And then a ceramics factory. My ceramics factory will be at the far end of the lake, so as to utilise the clay - the government has agreed; as they have to dig out the lake one day, we shall use the topsoil for the fields. First we'll remove all the pebbles (you know, there are hills over there), which can be used for construction. - it's a mine of pebbles. After removing the pebbles, there will be holes which then we'll fill with earth from the lake. And below this earth is a thick and compact layer of clay which is so hard it can't be used for farming - it's impossible - but it's wonderful for making ceramics. So right at the very end, in Indian territory, in Madras State, we'll have a large ceramics industry. On the other side, we'll have a little factory. for firing clay. All this is huge. A tremendous program. We can file it with the other things.

✳

On 23.6.65, while describing Her plan to develop "Auroville", Mother will comment:
"...in the Lake Estate project, there was already an airfield."
Two documents describing part of this "tremendous program" have now re-surfaced.

✳

An undated 16-page leaflet presenting Alexander Markey's project proposal is published by the Ashram and is entitled "NEW HORIZON International - motion pictures dedicated to a greater tomorrow". Among other things it says:

The 'Executive Producer' of the project is Dr. Alexander Markey. Chief architect of the New Horizon domain is Antonin Raymond of New York and Tokyo.

New Horizon International bas come into being for the specific purpose of meeting this challenge of our civilization. It is inspired by one of the most highly esteemed spiritual and cultural centres in the world and Is designed on a scale commensurate with the need. Its goal is the production of a constant flow of the kind of motion pictures that will foster a nobler, truer life for humanity.

New Horizon's entry into the field of motion picture production comprises a wide-scale program on a long-range basis. Its studios are designed to include facilities and equipment equal to the finest in the world in an atmosphere of inspiration and dedication.

Land has been acquired, building has begun and the "cornerstone" has been laid in the hearts and wills of those to whom this project has become an imperative.

Educational Films

An important part of the New Horizon program is a special department for the production of educational and inspirational films under the auspices of the Sri Aurobindo International faculty of the International University Centre; their production will conform to the standards of technical and creative excellence of all New Horizon films. These educational series are so conceived that they will lend themselves readily to adaptation into any desired language.

University Courses

It is the aim of the New Horizon management to provide every facility for talented youth from all parts of the world, particularly from India, who aspire to film careers. As the most effective means of achieving this, our program includes a comprehensive series of courses in every phase of motion picture production and management, under the auspices of the Sri Aurobindo International University Centre.

Model Township

Also within easy access to the studio, the project includes a township composed of a cluster of villages for local semiskilled and unskilled employees and their families.

Conceived as a unique little world, this community will preserve the commendable features of what is in the best Indian tradition, utilising at the same time modern conveniences, advantages and sanitary facilities, plus an element of beauty that could easily be adopted by other Indian rural communities without financial strain.

The township will have its own places of worship; municipal buildings; schools; recreational facilities, playground swimming pool; bazaar; community laundry; adult education and training centre; sewage disposal plant; electricity and uncontaminated drinking water for every home, and other conveniences and amenities.

**New Horizon will open
the way for mankind to a
new and truer life.**

Note that, in the welcoming message She read for Auroville's Inauguration Ceremony, Mother proclaimed "Are invited to Auroville all those who . . . aspire for a truer and higher life."

Note also that decades before her name of this project "New Horizon" re-surfaced, several Aurovilians had noted the similarities between Auroville and Akhet-Aton (literally "Horizon of the Aton"), the city built 33 centuries earlier by the Egyptian Pharaoh, Akhenaton at a site presently known as Amarna. Akhenaton tried to revolutionise the religion of his country by making it monotheist. This is very interesting because Mother explained that, in an earlier incarnation, She was Queen Tiye - that is Akhenaton's mother, who is said to have had a lot of influence on her son. Is this the reason why Mother named this attempt "New Horizon"?

✳

At least two Ashram connected businesses had "New Horizon" in their name.

- *On 12.4.57, Mother laid the foundation stone of the "New Horizon Sugar Mils" set up by the Hindocha family.*
- *Kishorilal Dhandania started the "New Horizon Stainless Steel" with Udar's help*

Could it be that, while She was hoping that Her "New Horizon" venture would take of, Mother included the words New Horizon" in the names of some businesses which hopefully would contribute to it?

New Year Message

1965

Salute to the advent of the Truth

**Salute to the
advent of the Truth**

The first sentence of "A Dream' *(in which She described, in 1954, an ideal society) is:* "There should be somewhere on earth a place which no nation could claim as its own.

Though there is no report in Auroville's Archives stating that, at this early stage, Mother spoke already of Her hope to have such a free territory for Auroville, it is likely to have been there at least in Her consciousness.

Her long-time wish was definitely not to separate Auroville from India (creating more divisions was definitely not part of Her program) but to have a territory free of private property/possession, free of money, free of all existing laws, rules and regulations (hence free of all existing taxes and duties) and free of the rule of any outside authority so that it is able to develop truly freely and create its own organisation and governance system, its own laws, rules, regulations, contribution system, its own judicial system, etc. all this according to its own evolving state of consciousness. For this to be at all possible, Auroville's territory would probably need to be quite large...

As more land is now required, it is decided to develop the township on both side of the NH 66 and not only on its west side.

Gilles Guigan, History of Autoville, Vol.1

Gilles Guigan, History of Autoville, Vol.1, Period ending on 28th February 1967, June 2016 version, A comprehensive compilation of Mother's known words and other documents, Auroville Archives

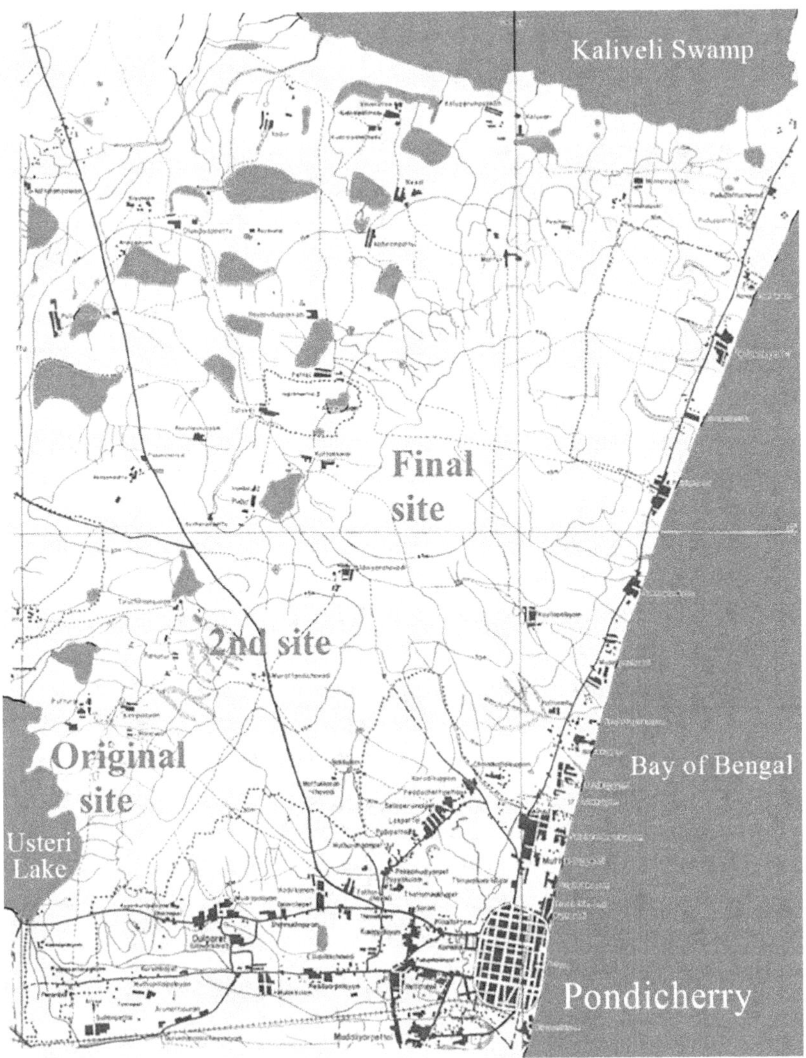

Map showing the first site for the Auroville construction (1964),
the second site (1965) and the final site (1966 onwards)

What are these powerful gods?

What are these powerful gods whose hour of manifestation upon earth has come, if not the varied and perfected modes of Thy infinite activity,

O Thou Master of all things, Being and Non-Being and What is beyond, Marvellous Unknowable One, our sovereign Lord? . . .

What are these manifold brilliant intellectual activities, these countless sunbeams illumining, conceiving and fashioning all forms, if not one of the modes of being of Thy infinite Will, one of the means of Thy manifestation,

O Thou Master of our destinies, sole unthinkable Reality, sovereign Lord of all that is and all that is not yet. . . .

And all these mental powers, all these vital energies, and all these material elements, what are they if not Thyself in Thy outermost form, Thy ultimate modes of expression, of realisation,

O Thou whom we adore devotedly and who escapest us on every side even while penetrating, animating and guiding us, Thou whom we cannot understand or define or name, Thou whom we cannot seize or embrace or conceive, and who art yet realised in our smallest acts. . . .

And all this enormous universe is only an atom of Thy eternal Will.

In the immensity of Thy effective Presence all things blossom!

The Mother, Prayers and Meditations, August 2nd 1914

Auroville 'Galaxy' Town Plan

Historical Aspects of Auroville

Although Auroville is a city to be built, the landscape in which it is situated has already had countless previous incarnations and avatars. Of special interest to future Aurovilians is the fact that a few miles away is its 'mother-town' Pondicherry, the home of Sri Aurobindo and The Mother, the site of the Sri Aurobindo Ashram.

The origins of Pondicherry go back into the night of time. Pondicherry means 'the new suburb'. The original name of the town, no longer used, was Vedapuri, and a big temple still stands today, the Vedapurishwara temple, dedicated to the great god Siva, the god of the contemplatives. Vedapuri means 'city of knowledge'. The patron saint of Vedapuri was Sri Agastya, legends of whose life tell of his coming from the far Himalayas, travelling south and settling in the country of the Tamils to teach the people the Veda. For thousands of years Vedapuri was a school for young Brahmins where they learned to chant the Vedic hymns in Sanskrit and to perform complicated sacrifices in the proper way.

Buddhism came and went, and then in the first and second centuries of our era we find on that same Coromandel Coast a Roman settlement mentioned in the Periple by Ptolemy of Alexandria. Heavily loaded ships from the far Mediterranean, swept by the constant trade winds, arrived via Cleopatra's Nile - Red Sea Canal at Poduke as our town was then called. A Roman emporium, a trader's town where Mediterranean wines and swords, Germanic slaves and Roman gold were exchanged for spices and silks, precious stones, cottons and peacocks of India. The poet-prince Ilango, brother of the Chera king Kovalan, describes how 'Auroville' appeared in the first century. The text is translated from the original picturesque Tamil.

Arial Auroville view of Matrimandir and the Matriamdir gardens.

"The sun shone over the open terraces, over the warehouses near the harbour, and over the turrets with their air-holes like the eyes of the deer (a description of windows built with a Roman arch). In different places the observer's attention was arrested by the sight of Yavanas (a name for Greeks and Romans) whose prosperity never waned.

"In the harbour were to be seen sailing vessels with many sailors from distant lands. To all appearances they lived as one community. In the streets of the city hawkers went about with cosmetics, bath powders, cool pastes, flowers, incense and fragrant perfumes. In certain places weavers were seen dealing in fine fabrics of silk, animal hair and cotton. Whole streets were full of cloth, corals, sandalwood and myrrh, besides a wealth of rare ornaments, perfect pearls, gems and gold beyond all reckoning."

The description of the city itself and the central highway leading to it also has its poetic charm: "Entering into the central highway of the city, rich with the wealth of sea-borne goods and reaching down to the seashore where flags of foreign countries fly high, one is impressed by these stretches of white sand where are displayed various kinds of goods brought in by ships of foreign merchants who have left their homes and settled here.

"Here, burning in the evening, were myriads of lamps: lamps of those who sold coloured powders, who sold sandalwood, jasmine flowers, scents, and all varieties of sweets; the lamps of dexterous goldsmiths, and of those who, sitting in a row, sold pittu; the broad black lamps placed on lampstands by the sellers of muffins; the lamps of fishmongers glimmering here and there; and high above all the bright beacon lights erected to guide ships to the shore. There were lamps taken out to sea by fishermen in their boats as they went with their nets, night-long lights set out by foreigners speaking strange languages, and finally the lamps lit by the watchmen of the warehouses containing valuable merchandise from far away countries."

Recent archaeological excavations of a hill called Arikamedu south of Pondicherry have yielded Greek and Roman coins and imported Mediterranean pottery, reminiscent of a trade very much to the detriment of the Roman empire. Such was the eagerness of Roman ladies to possess the colourful silks and fine muslins of India that Rome lost all its gold reserves in this exchange, but it benefited the kings of the Coromandel Coast, who became fabulously rich and were able to build the huge temple towns of Rameshwaram and Chidambaram, of Madurai and Trichinopoly, and - only a hundred miles from where Auroville is being built - the magnificent Versailles of India - Mahabalipuram.

Vedapuri itself fell asleep. The destructive force of Islam came and went; the Portuguese came and called the town 'Puducheira', and the Dutch, 'Poeleser', and the Danes - all trying to get some of the gold the Romans had lost, - and built their trading offices, their 'comptoirs'. In the 17th century came the French, who built on the shore the largest and most powerful fortress in southern India. As a fortress it was very successful, also as a safe place for investments in gold during troubled times. It quickly became rich, too rich for the jealous British in Madras, who razed it to the ground.

Rebuilt in the 18th century in the French provincial style, the town can be seen from the hills of Auroville, now a part of free India. Only a few small fishermen's villages without history stand today where the 20th century, with its big bulldozers, is moving in to build the city of a new dawn.

Medhananda, Equals One, City =1, Experiment Auroville, 1968

The Origins of Auroville

Auroville started her journey on 28th February 1968.

The Mother's Agenda, September 21st, 1966

'Even if you don't believe it, even if all the circumstances seem quite unfavourable, I KNOW THAT AUROVILLE WILL BE. It may take a hundred years, it may take a thousand years, but Auroville will be because it is DECREED.'

The Mother's Agenda, September 21st, 1966

In fact the Mother always spoke about Auroville as a place already existing, awaiting its time. She called it 'city the earth needs' and it is true that from earliest times the imagination of mankind has been haunted by the fabled names of lost cities or continents below the sea, places of spiritual power and material wealth. Myth and legend bear witness to this need of the human psyche for a place of transformation, for a sacred space where, as Joseph Campbell wrote, at any time the temporal walls may dissolve to reveal a wonder.

How far back must we go to find the true origins of Auroville? How long did this 'dream' lie dormant in the consciousness of the Mother? It was certainly there long before the foundation of the city in 1968. It was there before the first ever mention of the name;

Palmyra trees were the first and virtually only trees in the barren landscape.
Herdsmen and children guiding cows and goats
through the canyon landscape of early Auroville, 1968.

before the Mother reported her 'dream' to Surendranath Jauhar on the staircase leading to her room in the Ashram; even before her arrival in Pondicherry and her first meeting with Sri Aurobindo.

In the past there may have been attempts to manifest the ideal - how many we do not know. In conversation the Mother often referred to the 'cosmic tradition', a body of occult teachings transmitted by Max Théon.

This enigmatic personage had revived a Society called the Hermetic Brotherhood of Luxor, some of whose members attempted to found a spiritual community in America. The attempt was a failure. Nevertheless historians of the movement have made the connection with Auroville, even referring to it as 'that other step-child of Théon's - Auroville - founded by Mira Alfassa in 1968 to crown the success of the Pondicherry Ashram.'*

There are indications that the origins of Auroville, as a concept of the Mother, can be traced back to a remote past. On several occasions the Mother herself spoke of earlier incarnations in ancient Egypt. It is not surprising then that comparisons have been made between Auroville and the 'city of the horizon' built by Amenhotep IV (Akhenaten) in Upper Egypt around 1369-75 BCE. This city was remarkable in its conception and had a profound effect upon human consciousness in its place and time. The old gods of Egypt and their elaborate rituals were abolished in favour of a form of worship of the sun's disk seen as the symbol of life-giving energies that, unlike the old gods, were never represented in any human or animal shape. Like Auroville, Akhenaten's new city was dedicated to the service of Eternal Truth (Ma' at).

Its long-buried remains came to light only in 1887, when a peasant woman accidentally stumbled upon 300 cuneiform tablets. (Coincidentally, this was the year of the unsuccessful attempt made by the Brotherhood of Luxor to found a spiritually orientated community in America.) Many people have been struck by the similarity between the Auroville Charter and an inscription discovered at Ahkenaton's city:

**Here is the place that belongs to no prince,
to no god. Nobody owns it.
This is everybody's place. The earth will find joy in it.
Hearts will be happy in it.**

More than three thousand years later, on February 7th, 1968, The Mother defined the Charter of Auroville in strikingly similar terms when she wrote:

Auroville belongs to nobody in particular.

Auroville belongs to humanity as a whole.

Auroville wants to be the bridge between the past and the future.

In his book 'The Mother' Georges Van Vrekhem quotes the words of a French teacher at the Ashram school; 'In reply to this question (concerning Akhenaten) I had put to her, Mother let it clearly be understood that she had been Queen Tiye, the mother of Akhenaten... she specified that Akhenaten's revolution was intended to reveal to the people of that time the unity of the Divine and his manifestation. This attempt, the Mother added, was premature, for the human mind was not yet ready for it. It had, however, to be undertaken in order to ensure the continuity of its existence on the mental plane.'

If, as it seems, the idea of Auroville was latent in the Mother's consciousness even before her arrival in Pondicherry, it could not be realised concretely until two crucial events had taken place. The first was her meeting with Sri Aurobindo in March 1914, and the second the 'supramental descent' of February 1956, which her collaboration with Sri Aurobindo had made possible. Sri Aurobindo had told her: 'With the advent of the supramental force on earth, EVERYWHERE there will be a response'. At last, in 1956, the day came when the Mother could announce to the world: 'A new light breaks upon the earth.' A few years later she would issue her first public statement on Auroville: 'Auroville wants to be a universal town where men and women of all countries are able to live in peace and progressive harmony above all creeds, all politics and all nationalities. The purpose of Auroville is to realise human unity.'

The symbol chosen to represent Auroville was a circle divided into five segments. To some the five divisions represent personalities of the Universal Mahashakti described by Sri Aurobindo, including her personality of Ananda, which has never yet manifested on earth. Others have seen in it the five petals of the Plumeria flower, named by the Mother 'psychological perfection'. Many mysteries are contained in this ancient symbol, for we may also see that, within the circle, the lines take the shape of a five-pointed star around an inner ring with a dot in the centre. In ancient Egypt this hieroglyph was used to denote invisible energies of the spiritual realm. Each line radiating from the centre is like a line of force projecting the main thrust of the Auroville experiment towards its five-fold goal: that is, the discovery of the soul; the evolution of a new consciousness; the realisation of an actual human unity; peace on earth and the end of war; unending progress towards transformation and the 'life divine'. The five segments can be seen as representing an essential unity connecting each of these goals with the others at every point.

From the first, the plan of the new city - the galaxy design - reflected its cosmic significance. At the centre, the Matrimandir would rise like sun in the city of dawn, signifying the beginning of a new age. 'Matrimandir wants to be the symbol of the Divine's answer to man's aspiration for perfection' the Mother wrote. She also said that Matrimandir represented the Divine Consciousness, and that it would be Auroville's soul.

Numerous references in the Agenda suggest that the vision of Auroville did not come all of a piece, but was revealed to the Mother over a period of time. Surendra Nath Jauhar describes a meeting with the Mother on the staircase, when she told him about 'a wonderful dream'. The dream was written down and became the document we all know - 'There should be somewhere on earth a place that no nation could claim as its sole property; a place where all human beings of goodwill, sincere in their aspiration, could live freely as citizens of the world, obeying one single authority, that of the Supreme Truth.' This is perhaps the first direct reference to the future Auroville, but the time for the realisation of the dream had not yet come. A still earlier document, dating from 1953, contains the Mother's vision of a future 'international zone'. It forms part of a detailed proposal for a new International University Centre, in which the Mother's words are directly quoted:

'..the cultures of the different regions of the earth will be represented here in such a way as to be accessible to all, not merely intellectually in ideas, theories, principles and languages, but also vitally in habits and customs, in art under all forms.... and physically too through natural scenery, dress, games, sports, industries and food. A kind of world exhibition has to be organised in which all the countries will be represented in a concrete and living manner - the ideal is that every nation with a very definite culture would have a pavilion representing that culture, built on a model that most displays the habits of that country; it will exhibit the nation's most representative products, natural as well as manufactured, products that best express its intellectual and artistic genius and its spiritual tendencies'

The Mother always made it very clear that her ideal of unity had nothing to do with a featureless uniformity. Her ideal was a harmony and balance in which all the great achievements and aspirations of diverse cultural traditions would find their destined place within the whole. The participation of the entire world in the new venture was especially important to her. From the beginning, this universality was symbolised by the inauguration ceremony on 28th February 1968, when young people from 124 nations and all Indian states placed a handful of earth from their countries in a lotus-shaped urn. Soil from the Sri Aurobindo Ashram was carried by Nolini, emphasising the indissoluble bond between these two foundations presided over by the Mother.

The Agenda provides us with a fascinating insight into the Mother's vision of Auroville as it developed over time and reveals how closely it was linked with events in the world outside India. It should be remembered that at the time of Auroville's foundation, the 'Cold War' between Russia and the United States was at its height, and the threat of a nuclear catastrophe seemed ever present. On 21st September, 1966, the Mother voiced her concern about the world situation and the future role of Auroville. She spoke of her 'clear vision that Auroville was a centre of force and creation with, one could say, a grain of truth, and if it could expand and develop, the very movement of its growth would be a reaction against the catastrophic consequences of the arms race. It is interesting that there was no premeditation behind the birth of Auroville; it was simply, as it is always, a Force that acts, a kind of absolute that manifests, and it was so powerful...I obeyed an order, without thinking about it....' At that moment she saw clearly that the creation of Auroville would have an effect on the whole world, and what effect. It would be, she said, 'an action in the invisible'.

The mother's conception of Auroville was characterised by an inspired simplicity that often seemed at variance with the ideas of Auroville's pioneers, many of whom had brought with them all the political and cultural baggage of the world they had left behind. The creation of the Auroville Charter, as related in the Agenda on 7.2.68, is a wonderful example of her practical insight into the needs of the moment, seen in the light of an eternal Truth. She takes a black felt- tip pen and spells out in large letters the four points of the Charter; encompassing the aims and purpose of Auroville in words so exact and comprehensive, that nothing needs to be added and nothing can be taken away.

1. Auroville belongs to nobody in particular. Auroville belongs to humanity as a whole. But to live in Auroville one must be a willing servitor of the Divine Consciousness.

2. Auroville will be the place of an unending education, of constant progress and a youth that never ages.

3. Auroville wants to be the bridge between the past and the future. Taking advantage of all discoveries from without and from within, Auroville will boldly spring towards future realisations.

4. Auroville will be a site of material and spiritual researches for a living embodiment of an actual human unity.

When it was done, she said: 'It is not I who wrote that. I noticed something so interesting: it comes as an imperative, there's no discussion; I write it down, I HAVE TO write, whatever I do. And then, when it's gone it's gone! Even if I try to remember, it's gone! So it is clear that it does not come from here: it comes from above.'

Auroville is much more than the experiment in community living which the casual visitor sees. It is much more than the sum of its achievements up to the present. Its true origins are in the future as well as in the past, for it exists eternally in the Consciousness that embraces time and space. To this eternal dimension, to this vast potential for a transforming action 'in the invisible' we have as yet no access; we have not found the way. Sometimes we catch a glimpse when a little effort appears to produce results out of all proportion, just as Sri Aurobindo said that it would 'in the hour of God'. We see a small group of young people from opposing nations plant trees for peace in Auroville and the Berlin wall comes down and the prospect of war retreats into the background of human affairs. We are reluctant to believe there could be any connection - surely life is more complicated than that? But what if the 'complications' are a veil of falsehood, a fake 'reality' to which we all, somehow, consent? What if a new light breaking upon the world is using us to build a new consciousness?

Auroville is a way of getting things done, a new way that has never been available before. So what does it mean to be an Aurovilian? What is it that the Mother saw so clearly in her vision and wanted people to discover for themselves? She gave so much freedom to those who chose to build this new city - she did not ask them to be philosophers or yogis or saints, or even to have read Sri Aurobindo. She did not require any special skills or talents. She did not impose any rules of conduct or obligatory creeds. The Truth that Auroville serves is ever in movement and cannot be bound by regulations, it leads us on to endless adventures of self-discovery - how beautiful it is to live this Truth that is ageless!

The guidance given by the Mother to those who wanted to be Aurovilians emphasised first of all the need for the inner discovery. 'At the centre there is a being, free and vast and knowing, who awaits our discovery and who should become the active centre of our being and our life in Auroville.' All other guidance given by the Mother centres itself about one crucial point: 'the fulfilment of one's desires bars the way to the inner discovery which can only be achieved in the peace and transparency of perfect disinterestedness.' The conquest of desire - 'to unite with the Divine one must have conquered in oneself the very possibility of desire' is the key that opens the door to all the possibilities of the future. For ordinary human beings, it is perhaps the hardest task, for all are convinced of the validity of their desires.

In the absence of desires something happens: the possibility of contact with a Consciousness that is not limited or masked by our personal preferences. That consciousness is all-knowing and infinitely creative. The Mother brought it down to our human level and it is her legacy to Auroville.

Auroville is a mystery, and will remain so while our human mentality continues to prefer its endless debates, its preferred plans, its personal ambitions, to a simple action conceived in the mind's silence and carried out with perfect sincerity in a spirit of goodwill. As the Mother never tired of reminding us: 'La vraie chose et tellement simple' - reality is so simple.

Sonia Dyne

(From a talk given at the Auromira Centre, London, on 23.4.2006)
** The Hermetic Brotherhood of Luxor (1995) Godwin, Chanel & Deveney*

The Matrimandir, Banyantree and Amphitheatre in Auroville

The Matrimandir, a Sun Temple

The Matrimandir, a Sun Temple, dedicated to the Divine is the "Soul of Auroville" and symbol of Auroville's aspiration to the Divine.

The Matrimandir is located in the centre of Auroville, its all-white 12-sided marble-clad Inner Chamber - where a shaft of sunlight, or artificial light at night, focuses down onto a 70 cms diameter optical-quality glass sphere surrounded by 12 white columns - is a place for silent concentration.

The Matrimandir was conceived as a golden globe, somewhat flattened, as is the earth,
some 29 metres (94') high by 36 m.(117') in diameter.

The flattening makes the globe more like a torus with an interior vortex, as is the shape of the hyper-dimensional universe.

It was to be the body of the Divine Mother,
the Cosmic Mahashakti.

The Matrimandir

Towards the Sun

In Ancient Egypt they worshipped many gods. The Sun-God was called Aten. When Amenhotep IV became the Pharaoh he changed his name to Akhenaten, which means "One who serves Aten", the Sun God. He tried his best to change Egyptian worship of many gods into worship of only one god, the Sun God. Sri Aurobindo says that the Sun universally stands for the Supramental Truth, which is the New Consciousness that he and Mother brought for the earth and mankind.

History tells us that Akhenaten was strongly influenced by his mother, Queen Tiye, who we now know was Mother. Pharaoh Akhenaten moved the whole capital of Egypt from Thebes to a new city that he built, and there is even an inauguration date: February 22nd 1347 BCE (give or take a week or two). Akhenaten called his new city Akhet-Aten which means "City of the Horizon". We know that in the 1960's Mother planned to build her new city called "New Horizon" near Ustery Lake, Pondicherry.

Akhenaten founded his "City of the Horizon" with these words. "Here is the place that belongs to No person, No god. Nobody owns it. It is Everybody's place. The earth will find its Joy in it. Hearts will be Happy in it."

In 1968 AD, three thousand, three hundred and thirty seven years later, Mother founded Auroville. She said Auroville meant "City of Dawn". A city named for the time the sun comes up over the horizon. She used words very similar to the words Akhenaten used. Just like Akhenaten, Mother said "Auroville belongs to nobody in particular. Auroville belongs to humanity as a whole." Mother also called Auroville "The City the Earth needs." Akhenaten said, "The Earth will find its Joy in it." In his new City of the

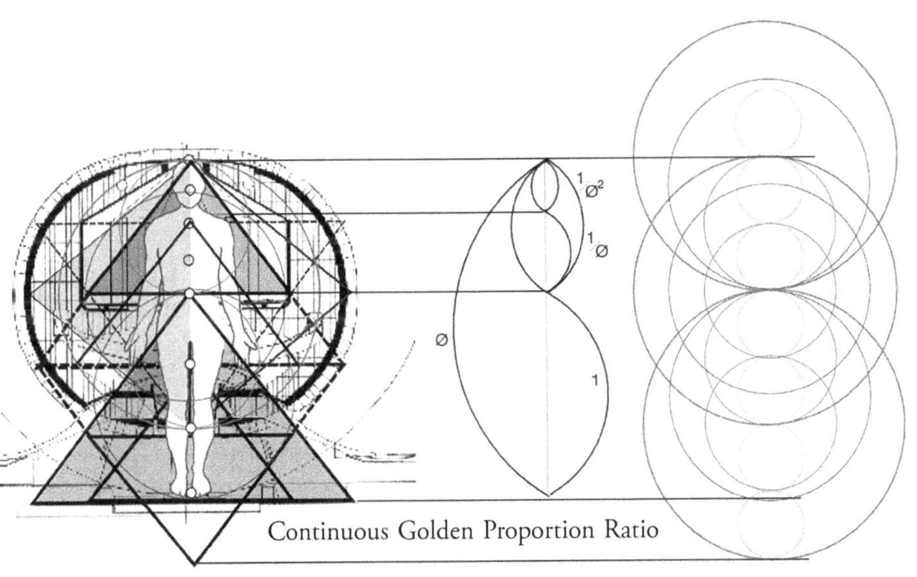

Continuous Golden Proportion Ratio

Stacked series of Vesucas in the Geometry of the Matrimandir

Great Pyramid Triangles in the Matrimandir

Connecting main points along the vertical axis with the circumferences of circles we find many great pyramid triangles in the design. The conclusion is that the Matrimandir is a spherical analogue of the Great Pyramid both geometrically and functionally. It, like pyramidal structures all over the world, creates a great vortex that conducts subtle energy into the earth. Modern science has found that there is a relationship between energy and form. Pyramids, for example, conform vortexes of measurable magnetic force. Other shapes have different energetics. The energy is in the angle.

The Mind Matrix, Robert Aaron Gulick, https://mind-matrix.net

Horizon, Pharaoh Akhenaten and his wife Queen Nefertiti built a temple to the Light. Up to that time, all Egyptian temples were filled with statues and paintings of gods and goddesses and people went there to worship their many gods. Akhenaten's new temple was empty inside. There were no statues, no paintings; nothing for traditional worship.

Mother put the Sun Temple Matrimandir in the centre of Auroville. She said the Matrimandir should not have any images or photographs and it should not be used for any form of worship or ritual. The Inner Chamber of the Matrimandir is lit by a ray of the sun at its centre. Akhenaten means one who serves the Sun God. We can see that long ago Akhenaten's Temple to the Light in his City of the Horizon was like Mother's Matrimandir in Auroville, her City of Dawn.

Mother explained that; "Akhenaten's revelation aimed at revealing to the humanity of that time the Unity of the Divine with its Manifestation."

This is the Unity that the new beings in Auroville will also realize - the eternal Divine Truth of Love that they are and the Divine Truth of that Love which is also our physical universe.

Mother said that Akhenaten's attempt was premature – men were not ready for it. She said that it had to be expressed more than three thousand years ago, so it would keep on living on the Mental Plane. It has been in the Universal Mind, which is open to everyone, and it has come down through time to us here in Auroville and to people all over the world. Akhenaten and Mother were doing the same work when they each built their city. Mother was helping Akhenaten build his city in Ancient Egypt when she was his mother, Queen Tiye.

- Loretta Shartsis

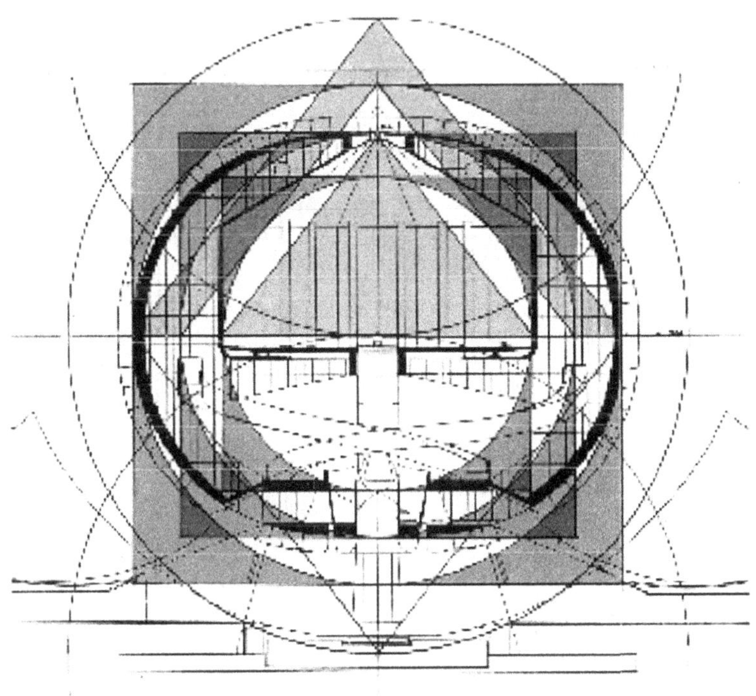

Harmonic geometric progression of the Great Pyramid Triangle and of Circles Squared in the Matrimandir.

The dimensions of the Inner Chamber match exactly the proportions of the Great Pyramid. Drawing then a larger triangle tangent to a circle equal to the diameter of the inner chamber will have a base equal to the diameter of the circle and equal to the height of the globe. Then yet again another Great Pyramid triangle will be tangent to that with a base equal to the width of the outer globe. The whole produces a harmonic progression of pyramid triangles and so also of circles squared.

The Mind Matrix, Robert Aaron Gulick, https://mind-matrix.net

The Inner Chamber of the Matrimandir

The Inner Chamber has been built exactly according to the vision of the Mother.

She described it to an Ashram engineer, Udar, who at her request made a measured drawing which she then passed on to the architect. She told him not to change anything and to include this Chamber in a larger building, which she said she had not 'seen'.

The Inner Chamber has a 12m radius (wall included). Its floor is covered with a white woollen carpet (except at the centre).

Its wall is 8.65 m. high. It has 12 facets which represent "the 12 months of the year" and are clad with white marble from Lasa, Italy.

Section and plan of the Inner Chamber:

Its white ceiling also has 12 facets, each one resting on one of the wall's facets and sloping by 30° upwards towards the centre. The Chamber's height at its centre is thus 15.2 m.

It has two double doors (located on opposite sides) made of thick white marble slabs. As wished by the Mother, the entrance door faces East. When closed, these doors are more or less invisible as she did not 'see' them in her vision.

It has 12 large steel cylindrical columns of 60cm diameter, covered with white lacquer, which the Mother had clearly 'seen' and which stand half-way between the centre of the room and each one of its 12 corners.

As their height is the same as that of the walls, they do not touch the ceiling and have no structural function.

As it has no windows, it is air-conditioned. The only light comes from a vertical beam of light, which the Mother wanted to be slightly golden and visible. This beam is normally a ray of the sun which is reflected down into the Chamber by a heliostat whose

The heliostat placed on top of the Matrimandir reflects a ray of sunlight
down into the Chamber to touch the Crystal at the centre.
From there the sun ray travels through the Crystal,
through an aperture in the floor of the Chamber to a Lotus Pond
underneath the structure, which connects 'Heaven with Earth'.

computerised tracking system keeps it very precisely oriented. Electrical spotlights create a similar effect at night and on cloudy days.

At the centre of the room, there is the object of concentration upon which falls a single vertical beam of sunlight.

This object is a crystal globe (70cm diameter, 400kg) custom-made of optically perfect glass in Germany by 'Schott' and later polished by 'Zeiss'.

It rests on a 'cube stand' (35cm side) consisting of 4 upright gilded symbols of Sri Aurobindo that hold each other up by the points of their triangles.

This 'cube' stands at the centre of the room on a 3m diameter symbol of the Mother, which is engraved in a white marble slab.

The crystal globe is positioned exactly at the flattened sphere's centre.

The Mother stressed that "the important thing is the play of the sunbeam on the centre. Because that becomes a symbol – the symbol of the future realisation."

The Inner Chamber is a place meant for concentration, to "learn how to concentrate" with a view to try to finding one's consciousness.

The 70-cm optically perfect glass globe at the heart of the
Matrimandir's Inner Chamber is illuminated
by a focused beam of light from above.

This sun ray travels down, through the different levels of the structure,
to touch the Lotus Pond below,
completing the link between Spirit and Matter.

Individual and Collective Soul

The individual has a soul. Likewise a collection of individuals, a group too has a soul. When persons habitually meet together for a certain purpose, they form a set or society and gradually tend to develop a common consciousness which is the beginning of a soul. At school, they who read together, the class, they who play together, the team, all who live and move together inspired by the same or similar impulses and ideas possess a rudimentary soul. In the same way, a bigger group, the nation has also a soul, each its own according to its nature, tradition and culture. Even a continent has a soul. One can speak of the soul consciousness of Europe, of Asia or of Africa. Indeed each cell of an organism has a consciousness of its own; it may be said to be the unit individual consciousness. Many such cells combine to form the organism, the individual (who in this way may be viewed as a composite or collective being). Many individuals form the family – each family with its group consciousness (whence the idea of kuladharma, the genius of the family or the tradition and stamp of a Royal House). Many families formed the tribe, here too each with its particular consciousness. And then families and tribes have formed the modern nation, each one a distinct and almost a well-developed soul. The grouping continues to enlarge and we have the many nations combining to form the human group as a whole; humanity too has its own consciousness and its own soul. There is no limit to the volume or dimension of the group. The earth has its soul consciousness, even as the sun or a star or any other planet. The solar system or a galactic system too is moved by its own secret consciousness.

Nolini Kanta Gupta, Collected Works 1972, Book 3, p. 231

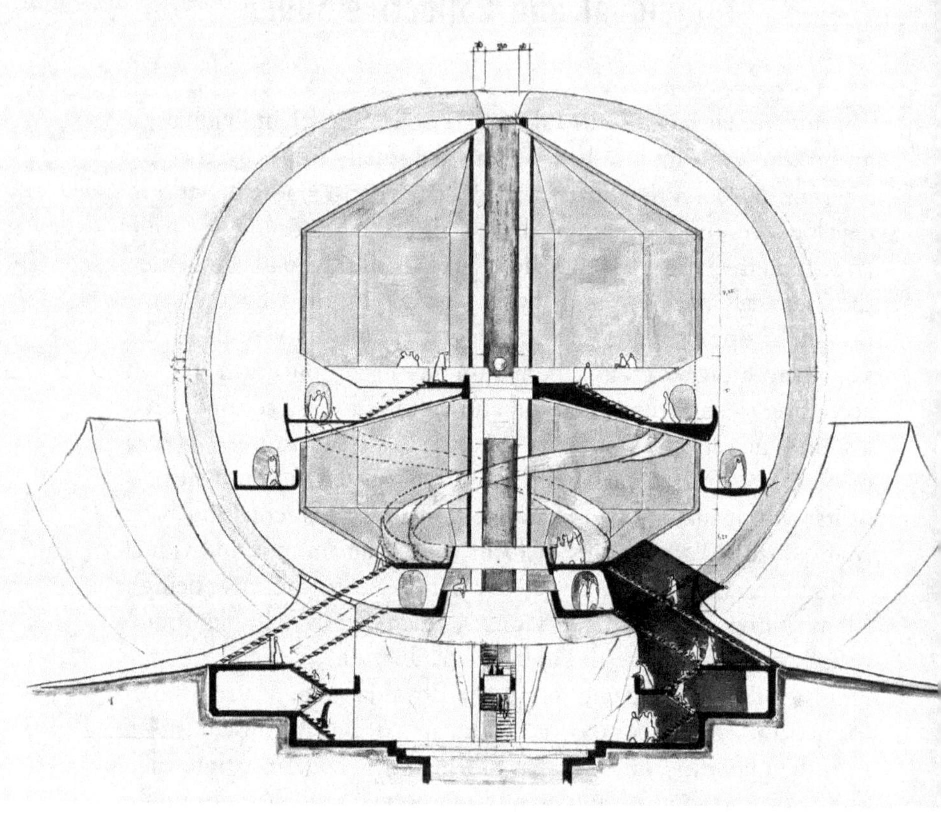

Sphere	36 m dia, 29 m height
Petals	at 6.50 m height extending to a 49 m radius
Foundations	10 m below ground level
Inner Chamber	24 m dia
	15.20 m height at centre
	8.65 m height of walls
	8.65 m height of columns
Crystal	0.70 m dia

Earth a Symbol

The Earth is the centre of the material universe. It has been created for concentrating the force that is to transform Matter. It is the symbol of the divine potentiality in Matter. As we have said, the Earth was created through a direct intervention of the Divine Consciousness: it is on the Earth alone that there is and can be the direct contact with the Divine. The Earth absorbs and develops and radiates the divine light; its radiation spreads through space and extends wherever there is Matter. The material universe shares, to some extent, the gift that the Earth brings – the light and harmony of the Divine Consciousness. But it is upon the Earth alone that there is the full and final flowering of that consciousness.

The psychic being is found on the Earth alone, for it is a product of the Earth: it is the touch of the Divine upon Matter. The psychic being is a child of the Earth: it is born and grows upon Earth, it is native to nowhere else. Still when it develops sufficiently and becomes an adult individuality, it can go to other physical domains, visit other planets, for example.

Nolini Kanta Gupta, Collected Works 1972, Book 3, p. 228
The Yoga of Sri Aurobindo

Body, the Occult Agent

The body has an individuality of its own. It is an organised formation and acts as a whole in each and all its parts. The human body is, *par excellence,* such a formation; for it is moved and controlled by the consciousness which overshadows or informs it, which is its master, whose will it executes scrupulously.

The body is an epitome of the world. It encases within its frame the whole world, particularly the Earth – Earth itself being an epitome of the world – on a miniature scale, the *mikros* reproducing all the features and characters of the *makros.*

Such being the case, a wholly conscious body governed and inspired by the supreme Consciousness lives and moves in the cosmic rhythm: not only does it register in itself the world happenings, but also possesses an active power to control and even to change those happenings by its individual movement. We may imagine the body to be a kind of map or chart of the Earth. Each spot on the Earth is represented by a particular spot – a certain group of cells, for example – in the body. If the consciousness ruling the body concentrates itself upon that point and induces a change there, a corresponding change can be brought about automatically on a larger scale in the part and conditions of the Earth with which it is connected. Thus without going out and moving about, without being the "man on the spot" to know things "at first hand", one can, sitting, in one's room, by switching on a key, as it were, in one corner of the body, set in movement a whole process of happenings in a particular region of the Earth. By a conscious re-disposition of a few cells in your body, you can bring about a desired change in world circumstances. The body is thus a control room for the consciousness in respect of happenings upon Earth. Naturally, any body cannot do that, but only a body destined and trained for that purpose.

A body, in this way, becomes the instrument, a lever for producing mighty changes and creations upon Earth. This conception of the occult potency of the body is at the basis of the rite or institution of sacrifice that was a characteristic feature of the old-world society. Iphigenia was offered as a victim to avert the wrath of the gods and bring victory to the Greeks. Sometimes an animal replaced the human victim and served the same purpose and in the same way. And in a higher sense – indeed in the highest sense – a body can sacrifice itself in such a way – wholly and integrally – as to bring about a corresponding integral reversal or revaluation in the physical world. A human being that makes of himself a holocaust – burns himself out at the altar of the Divine – keeping nothing for his own sake, living for the Divine alone, by calling down the divine will in himself, brings into the earthly life too a divine presence and transformation. A total physical sacrifice results inevitably into a total expression and embodiment of the Divine in the Physical world.

Nolini Kanta Gupta, Collected Works 1972, Book 3, p. 245
The Yoga of Sri Aurobindo

The Two Chains of the Mother

Well, I have talked a lot in my rather long life, have I not? I have talked a good deal, written much more.

All that forms now my Collected Works: eight volumes in English and as many volumes in Bengali.

All of you are leaving our Centre of Education, a Centre where you have been for so many years. To complete your course and come out of the Centre, it's all right; but to go where?

It seems you have already come to a decision, there are many amongst you who have made their choice. That's good, for it means choosing one's life.

I wanted to tell you only one thing: you are going out but wherever you go, you carry something within you, something that is permanent and eternal since the beginning of the world.

I have sometimes spoken of the golden chain of the Mother; I have said too that Mother had two chains, one of gold and the other of iron. These two chains are your eternal companions; wherever you may go, you will carry these two with you. You are bound to the Mother forever - forever, be sure of that. It's the prop of your life, it's your aspiration.

These are not chains of bondage but of freedom and entire satisfaction. You may ask: what are these chains of gold and of iron? The golden chain is in your soul and the iron one is in your body. The body, your body, is also bound to the Mother, to her Presence and Influence. Body means not only the material body, but the physical body, the inner body.

Now, the imprint of the Mother's Presence, you carry that in this physical body. You may not be always aware of that, but this makes no difference, nothing at all. Here I may refer to something pertinent.

One day someone went to see the Mother on his birthday; it was our Prithwi Singh. Now, Prithwi Singh plaintively said to the Mother: "Mother, here I am, so near to you; it's my birthday, a day so nice and precious to me, but I cannot see you, for I am blind in both of my eyes." Then the Mother answered: "What does that matter? You cannot see me but I am seeing you."

And this is always so. You cannot see with your physical eyes but the Mother's look is always upon you, her look of love and protection: be sure and certain of that. You carry that within you for all time and wherever you go, wherever in the entire world. You carry in you a portion, a spark of her Love; and that will save you from many difficulties, from much danger.

If you can keep that in your active memory, it will be still more beneficial. That's all.

A talk to the outgoing students of the International Centre of Education
Sri Aurobindo Ashram, on 25-10-1978.
Nolini Kanta Gupta, Collected Works, Book 8, Vedic Hymns

The Great Past ought to be followed by a Greater Future.

June 7th, 1967, Mother:

Then I would like to publish this quotation from Sri Aurobindo:

The traditions of the past are very great in their own place, in the past, but I do not see why we should merely repeat them and not go farther. In the spiritual development of the consciousness upon earth the great past ought to be followed by a greater future.

✳

Use the past as a springboard to leap towards the future.

Darshan of Sri Aurobindo and the Mother
Pondicherry, 24th April 1950

The whole world is my seraglio

and every living being

and inanimate existence in it

is the instrument of my rapture.

Sri Aurobindo

Photo References

List of contributors

List of References

Sri Aurobindo, Isha Upanishad, CWSA 17, pp 130-132   Page 15-16

Nolini Kanta Gupta, Collected Works, Book 8, p.10   18-19

Sri Aurobindo, Essays Divine and
Human with Thoughts and Aphorisms, pp. 149 - 153   21-24
Sri Aurobindo Ashram, Pondicherry, 1994

Sri Aurobindo, Letters on Yoga, Spiritual Evolution and the Supramental   25-30

Sri Aurobindo, Essays Divine and Human, pp. 149-153   32-33

Sri Aurobindo, The Secret of the Veda, SABCL, Vol. 10   35-36

Sri Aurobindo, Secret of the Veda, Rig-veda, SABCL, Vol. 10   37

Sri Aurobindo, The Secret of the Veda, SABCL, Vol. 10   39

Sri Aurobindo, Essays Divine and Human, 90, 91, 92, pp. 301-384   40-45

Sri Aurobindo, The Secret of the Veda, Letters on Yoga - III, Book III,
The Opening of the Inner Senses,
https://incarnateword.in/cwsa/30/sun-moon-star-fire   46-47

Sri Aurobindo, Essays Divine and Human, pp. 165-168,
Record of Yoga, Vol. 10   48-51
https://motherandsriaurobindo.in/Sri-Aurobindo/books/record-of-yoga/

Sri Aurobindo, Record of Yoga, Vol. 10, The Hour of God,
The Absolute and the Manifestation   52-54

Sri Aurobindo, The Hour of God, Section III,
The Absolute and the Manifestation (Record of Yoga, Vol. 10)   55
Sri Aurobindo Ashram, Pondicherry, 1959

Seven Jewel of the Mother Earth, Michael Miovic,   56
Savitri Bhavan, Auroville Radio, Auroville, 16th August 2012

Sri Aurobindo, The Hour of God, Section III, The Absolute and the
Manifestation, p.87, (Record of Yoga, Vol. 10)   58
Sri Aurobindo Ashram, Pondicherry, 1959

Amal Kiran (K.D. Sethna), The Sun and The Rainbow, Clear Ray Trust,
Pondicherry, 1981   65-66

Sri Aurobindo, 13th October 1939, CWSA, Collected Poems   67

Bibliography

Essays Divine and Human with Thoughts and Aphorisms, Sri Aurobindo 1994,
Sri Aurobindo Ashram Trust, Pondicherry, India

Prayers and Meditations, Volume 1, Collected Works of The Mother
The Mother, 2003, Sri Aurobindo Ashram Trust, Pondicherry, India

Collected Works of Nolini Kanta Gupta, 1979
Sri Aurobindo International Centre of Education, Pondicherry

Mother Agenda, Institut de Recherches Evolutives, Paris,
Mira Aditi, Mysore, India

The Beginning of History for Israel, 1995
The Integral Life Foundation, P.O. Box 239, Waterford CT. 06385, U.S.A.
Printed at Sri Aurobindo Ashram Press, Pondicherry, India

The Pyramids and the Sphinx, as seen by the Ancient Egyptians in
Hieroglyphic Inscriptons, Medhananda, Identity Research Institute,
2006, SABDA, Pondicherry, India

The Royal Cubit, Psychometrics of Ancient Egypt, Medhananda,
Identity Research Institute, 2006, SABDA, Pondicherry, India

The Ancient Egyptian Senet Game, The Game of Archetypes, Medhananda
Identity Research Institute, 2006, SABDA, Pondicherry, India

Archetype of Liberation, Psychodynamics of Ancient Egypt, Medhananda,
2006, Identity Research Institute, 2006, SABDA, Pondicherry, India

The Way of Horus, The Pictoriaol Way of Ancient Egypt, Medhananda, 2006
Identity Research Institute, 2006, SABDA, Pondicherry, India

Sur les Sentiers Solaires (On Solar Path), Ou l'Histoire pas comme les autres,
2008, Paul Vincent Baptiste, Edilivere, France

The Ancient Secret of the Flower of Life, Vol. 1 & Vol. 2, April 1, 1999
Light Technology Publishing, Drunvalo Melchizedek

Akhenaten, King of Egypt, Cyril Aldred
1998 Thames and Hudson Ltd, London, First edition 1991

Amarna, City of the Sun God, 2023, Ny Carlsberg Glyptotek

When Women Ruled the World, Six Queens of Egypt, Kara Cooney, 2020
National Geographic Partners, Washington, D.C.

Amarna, Guide to the Ancient City of Akhetaten,
The American University in Cairo Press, First published in 2020

Egypt's Golden Couple, When Akhenaten and Nefertiti were Gods on Earth,
St. Martin's Press, New York, First edition 2022, John Darnell and
Colleen Darnell

The Complete Gods and Goddesses of Ancient Egypt, 2017
Thames & Hudson, Richard H. Wilkinson

Books of the Dead, 1994, Manuals for Living and Dying,
Thames and Hudson, Stanislav Grof

Tantra Art, Council of Great Britain, Hayward Gallery, London, 1971
Ait Mookerjee, Director of Crafts Museum, New Delhi

The Complete Gods and Goddesses of Ancient Egypt, 2017
Thames & Hudson, Richard H. Wilkinson

Books of the Dead, 1994, Manuals for Living and Dying
Thames and Hudson, Stanislav Grof

The Sirius Mystery, New Scientific Evidence of Alien Contact 5,000 Years Ago,
Destiny Books, 1998, Robert Temple

Pharaos of the Sun
Akhetaten, Nefertiti, Tutankhamen, Museum of Fine Arts, Boston, 1999

Im Licht von Amarna, Ägyptisches Museum und Papyrussammlung, 2012

Hermann A. Schlögl, Nofretete, Die Wahrheit über die schöne Königin
C.H. Beck Wissen, 2013

Hermann A. Schlögl, Echnaton, C.H. Beck Wissen, 2008

Echnaton, Sonnenhymnen, Ägyptisch / Deutsch
Philipp Reclam jun. Stuttgart, 2007

Offizieller Katalog, Die Hauptwerke im Ägyptischen Museum Kairo
Arabische Republik Ägypten, 1986

The Woman who would be King, Hatshepsut's Rise to Power in Ancient Egypt
Kara Cooney, 2014, B\D\W\Y, Broadway Books, New York

The Silver Eye, Unlocking the Pyramid Texts
Susan Brind Morrow, 2016, Head of Zeus Ltd

Nofretete und Echnaton, Ein Herrscherpaar im Glanz der Sonne, Christian
Jacq, 2000, Rowohlt Taschenbuch Verlag

Amarna Sunset, Nefertiti, Tutankhamun, Ay, Horemheb, and the Egyptian
Counter-Reformation, Aidan Dodson, 2009
The American University in Cairo Press, Cairo, New York

Son of the Sun, by Savitri Devi, 2015
Supreme Grand Lodge Of The Ancient and Mystical Order Rosae Crucis

La Demeure du rayonnant - Mémoires égyptiennes, Daniel Meurois
Editions le Passe-Monde, 2011

Das Geheimnis des Aton, Daniel Meurois, Silberschnur Verlag, 2018

When Woman ruled the World, Six Queens of Egypt, Kara Cooney
National Geographic, 2014

Earth Grids, The Secret Patterns of Gaia's Sacred Sites
Hugh Newman, First published 2008, Published by Wooden Books Ltd,
Glastonbury, Somerset

Moses and Akhenaten, The Secret History of Egypt at the Time of the Exodus
Ahmed Osman, Published by Bear & Company,
Rochester, Vermont, 1990, 2002

The Mind Matrix, Robert Aaron Gulick, https://mind-matrix.net

Amarna Project
www.amarnaproject.com/pages/amarna_the_place/boundary_stelae/index.shtml